the
LAST DAYS of the
'DELTICS'

CRAIG W. FELLOWS & PAUL E. GASH

D1702981

LONDON
IAN ALLAN LTD

Preface

The 'Deltic'-hauled special train which ran from Kings Cross to Edinburgh and back on 2 January 1982 marked the last appearance of this type of locomotive in operation on British Rail. During the previous months the 'Deltics' had commanded a cult enthusiast following not seen on British Rail since the end of steam, surpassing even that of the demise of the 'Westerns' in 1976/77. This book tells the story of those last few months and explains the background of the various operational decisions that were made towards the end of the 'Deltic Era'. We would like to thank our friends and colleagues for their assistance in the preparation of this book. It is our own personal tribute to a great and sadly-missed locomotive.

'Tis now the death Class Fifty-Five,
The cutters torch you won't survive,
Your reputation is unmarred,
Standing in the breakers yard.

Cover:
No 55.010 *The King's Own Scottish Borderer* stands in York station on 21 November 1981. *R. Sutcliffe*

Previous page:
The 'Deltic Cumbrian' railtour at Dent on 14 November. *J. S. Whiteley*

Below:
55.015 *Tulyar* crosses Ribblehead viaduct on 5 December 1981 with the 'Hadrian Flyer' railtour, the last 'Deltic' working over the Settle & Carlisle line. *D. B. Stacey*

Contents

First published 1986

ISBN 0 7110 1555 4

Published by Ian Allan Ltd, Shepperton, Surrey; and printed by Ian Allan Printing Ltd at their works at Coombelands in Runnymede, England

1 The Final Months of Operation

At the end of September 1981 the last three power-units for the 'Deltic' fleet were being reconditioned at Doncaster Works. On 28 September three locomotives each lost an engine, and the policy of cannibalisation of power-units from one 'Deltic' to another loomed nearer. The first of the three locomotives to be restricted to 'one engine' was 55.019 at Haymarket depot. After working the previous night's 22.15 Kings Cross-Aberdeen train it was found to have number two engine de-phased, but nevertheless, even restricted to 'one engine', it was put to work on the 07.18 Edinburgh-Carlisle train. The second locomotive to lose an engine that day was 55.021 whilst working the 14.15 York-Kings Cross train; it failed at Selby and had to be driven from the rear cab back to York depot. Examination found that number one engine was de-phased, and so a 'one engine' restriction was placed on the locomotive. The third 'Deltic' to suffer a power-unit failure was 55.011: whilst working the 20.19 York-Kings Cross train number two power-unit kept shutting down. Examination at Finsbury Park found a broken ball race in the chip trap and a 'one engine' restriction was placed on the locomotive. (Further inspection at York depot on 10 October found that the quill shaft had disintegrated in number two engine.)

The following day, 29 September, 55.014 emerged from Doncaster Works after a power-unit change, and two days later 55.010 was released back into traffic after having a split oil collector drum repaired on number one engine. Friday 2 October saw the last 'Deltic' visits to Cleethorpes, with 55.021 working the 08.30 from Kings Cross and 13.05 return, while 55.011 worked the 13.05 from London and 17.45 return, both locomotives restricted to one engine. Also on this date 55.009 ran light engine from Edinburgh to North Berwick to assist a North Berwick-Edinburgh dmu which had failed. The following day 55.007 visited Perth with an Edinburgh-Kyle of Lochalsh SRPS excursion, and 55.019 ran light diesel from York to Barrow Hill for Barrow Hill's 'open day'. (55.019 was chosen because of its one engine restriction.)

In the early part of October it was decided that the three power-units being reconditioned at Doncaster Works would be reserved for 'Deltics' Nos 11, 19 and 21. On the 5 October 55.021 was sent to Doncaster Works for a power-unit change, followed the next day by 55.019. This just left 55.011 running in traffic on one engine, waiting to be called to Doncaster for the last reconditioned power-unit the works was to overhaul and replace, but sadly 55.011's call never came. 55.021 returned to traffic on 16 October, but 55.019 had quite a lengthy stay, not returning until 10 November.

Monday 5 October saw the commencement of the winter timetable, and with the further introduction of High Speed Train sets and cutbacks in services, there were now only five diagrams allocated to Class 55 haulage on Mondays to Fridays, only four on Saturdays and just three on Sundays. These were as follows:

Below:
The beginning of the end: the remains of *Nimbus*, the first 'Deltic' to be broken up, at Doncaster Works on 18 January 1980. *P. E. Gash*

Below right:
The last 'Deltic' at Cleethorpes: 55.011, on one engine, waits to depart with the 17.45 to Kings Cross on 2 October 1981. *C. W. Fellows*

3

Monday to Friday
Winter Diagrams
Commencing 5 October 1981

No 1
Off 5
Class 55

TRAIN WORKING	ARR	DEP	WTT NO	DAYS RUN
Doncaster	00.21 RR	00.40	5L04	MSX
Clifton CS	01.18		0L01	
York depot	01.28			
FUEL				
York depot		06.55	0A08	SX
Clifton CS (EH)		07.30	5A08	
York	07.35	08.07	1A08	
Kings Cross	11.05	11.40	0B02	
Fin Park depot	12.00			
FUEL				
Fin Park depot		15.33	0L44	
Kings Cross (EH)		16.03	1L44	
York	19.04		0A34	
York (EH)		20.19	1A34	
Kings Cross	23.26	23.55	0B02	
Fin Park depot	00.15			
FUEL				
Works 2				

No 2
Off 1
Class 55

TRAIN WORKING	ARR	DEP	WTT NO	DAYS RUN
Fin Park depot		05.20	0S12	SX
Kings Cross		05.50	1S12	
Newcastle	10.19		0L01	
York depot				
FUEL				
York depot		14.45	0A26	
Clifton CS (EH)		15.00	5A26	
York	15.05	15.50	1A26	
Kings Cross	18.59	19.40	0B02	
Fin Park depot	20.00			
FUEL				
Fin Park depot		21.45	0S70	
Kings Cross (EH)		22.15	1S70	
Edinburgh	04.19	04.24	0G99	
Haymarket depot	04.31			
FUEL				
Works 3				

No 3
Off 2
Class 55

TRAIN WORKING	ARR	DEP	WTT NO	DAYS RUN
Haymarket depot		09.15	0V93	SX
Edinburgh (EH)	09.22	09.50	1V93	
York	13.20			
York (EH)		14.34	1S27	
Edinburgh	17.59	18.04	0G99	
Haymarket depot	18.11			
FUEL				
Haymarket depot		19.50	0E35	
Edinburgh (SH)	19.57	20.25	1E35	
Kings Cross	04.45	05.25	0B02	MX
Fin Park depot	05.45			
FUEL				
Works 4				

No 4
Off 3
Class 55

TRAIN WORKING	ARR	DEP	WTT NO	DAYS RUN
Haymarket depot		23.32	0E43	SUO
Edinburgh (SH)	23.39	00.07	1E43	MO
Kings Cross	07.15	08.21	0B02	
Fin Park depot	08.41			
FUEL				
Fin Park depot		13.33	0L43	SX
Kings Cross (EH) (Z)		14.03	1L43	
York	17.01		0A31	
York (EH) (Z)		18.14	1A31	
Kings Cross	21.32	21.35	0B02	
Fin Park depot	22.15			
FUEL				
Works 5				
(Z) (SH) FO				

No 5
Off 4
Class 55

TRAIN WORKING	ARR	DEP	WTT NO	DAYS RUN
Fin Park depot		09.10	0L41	SX
Kings Cross (EH)		09.40	1L41	
York	12.52		0L01	
York Depot	13.07			
FUEL				
York depot		13.55	0A22	
York (EH)		14.15	1A22	
Kings Cross	17.26	18.23	0D08	
Kings Cross (EH)	(18.59)	19.40	1D08	
Hull	23.13RR	23.30	5L04	
Doncaster	00.21RR	00.40	5L04	MX
Works 1				

Saturday
Winter Diagrams
Commencing 10 October 1981

TRAIN WORKING	ARR	DEP	WTT NO	DAYS RUN
No 1				
Off 6				
Class 55				
Doncaster	00.21 RR	00.40	5L04	SO
Clifton CS	01.18		0L01	
York depot	01.28			
FUEL				
York depot		06.55	0A08	SO
Clifton CS (EH)		07.30	5A08	
York	07.35	08.07	1A08	
Kings Cross	11.05	11.40	0B01	
Kings Cross Standage	11.50			
Kings Cross Standage		15.43	0L44	
Kings Cross (EH)		16.03	1L44	
York	19.04	19.15	5L44	
Clifton CS	19.20		0D01	
York depot	19.30			
FUEL				
Works 5				

Below:
The end for *Ballymoss*: 55.018 at Doncaster on 12 October 1981 being removed from the 19.40 Kings Cross-Hull train. *D. B. Stacey*

TRAIN WORKING	ARR	DEP	WTT NO	DAYS RUN
No 2				
Off 1				
Class 55				
Fin Park depot		05.20	0S12	SO
Kings Cross		05.50	1S12	
Newcastle	10.19		0L01	
York depot				
FUEL				
York depot		14.45	0A26	
Clifton CS (EH)		15.00	5A26	
York	15.05	15.50	1A26	
Kings Cross	18.59	19.31	0B02	
Fin Park depot	19.51			
FUEL				
Works 1				

TRAIN WORKING	ARR	DEP	WTT NO	DAYS RUN
No 3				
Off 2				
Class 55				
Haymarket depot		09.15	0V93	SO
Edinburgh (EH)	09.22	09.50	1V93	
York	13.20			
York (EH)		14.34	1S27	
Edinburgh	17.59	18.04	0G99	
Haymarket depot	18.11			
FUEL				
Works 3				

TRAIN WORKING	ARR	DEP	WTT NO	DAYS RUN
No 4				
Off 3				
Class 55				
Fin Park depot		13.33	0L43	SO
Kings Cross (EH)		14.03	1L43	
York	17.01		0A31	
York (EH)		18.14	1A31	
Kings Cross	21.32	22.00	0B02	
Fin Park depot	22.20			
FUEL				
Works 2				

TRAIN WORKING	ARR	DEP	WTT NO	DAYS RUN
No 5				
Off 4				
Class 55				
Spare, Fin Park depot				SO
Works 4				

Sunday
Winter Diagrams
Commencing 11 October 1981

TRAIN WORKING	ARR	DEP	WTT NO	DAYS RUN
No 1				
Off 2				
Class 55				
Fin Park depot		13.35	0L42	SUO
Kings Cross (EH)		14.05	1L42	
York	17.19			
York (EH)		19.13	1A19	
Kings Cross	22.09	22.51	0B02	
Fin Park depot	23.11			
FUEL				
Works 2				

TRAIN WORKING	ARR	DEP	WTT NO	DAYS RUN
No 2				
Off 4				
Class 55				
Fin Park depot		09.35	0L41	SUO
Kings Cross (EH)		10.05	1L41	
York	13.18		0L01	
York depot	13.33	15.30	0A10	
York (EH)		15.50	1A10	
Kings Cross	19.44			
FUEL				
Fin Park depot		21.45	0S70	
Kings Cross (EH)		22.15	1S70	
Edinburgh	04.19	04.24	0G99	MO
Haymarket depot	04.31			
FUEL				
Works 3				

TRAIN WORKING	ARR	DEP	WTT NO	DAYS RUN
No 3				
Off 3				
Class 55				
Haymarket depot		10.50	OV93	SUO
Edinburgh (EH)	10.57	11.25	1V93	
York	15.14		OL01	
York depot	15.29	17.10	OS27	
York (EH)		17.30	1S27	
Edinburgh	21.14	21.19	OG99	
Haymarket depot	21.26			
FUEL				
Works 4				

TRAIN WORKING	ARR	DEP	WTT NO	DAYS RUN
No 4				
Off 5				
Class 55				
Spare, Fin Park depot				SUO
Works 5				

TRAIN WORKING	ARR	DEP	WTT NO	DAYS RUN
No 5				
Off 1				
Class 55				
Spare, York depot				SUO
Works 1				

Below:
Running on one engine, 55.011 passes through Henwick Hall on 9 October 1981 with the 15.50 York-Kings Cross train. *P. M. Marsh*

It is worth noting that originally the 'Deltic' locomotive programmes issued involved an extra diagram on each weekday, and two on Sundays. On Monday to Saturday this involved the 'Deltic' number five diagram; instead of taking 5L04 stock from Hull to York, it went light engine to Doncaster to work the 03.55 Doncaster-Hull train, and then worked 1A13, the 09.36 Hull-Kings Cross, and 1L45, the 17.40 (18.05 on Saturdays) Kings Cross-York; it would then carry on to work programme number one. On Sunday 'Deltics' were allocated to the 11.50 York-Kings Cross and 1L43 16.05 Kings Cross-York services. But as another High Speed Train was made available these original diagrams were not implemented.

On 5 October whilst undergoing a D examination at York, 55.018 had its boiler officially condemned after being examined by the District Boiler Inspector. This meant that 'Deltic' No 18 was restricted to electric train heating only. With only three months left before the withdrawal of the whole class, it was not practicable to have a new boiler fitted: this was the beginning of the end for *Ballymoss*.

At the beginning of October the CM&EE at York gave instructions that York depot was to prepare four 'Deltics' to work a series of 'Deltic' specials being organised. The locomotives chosen were 55.002, 55.009, 55.015 and 55.022, and they had to be in first class condition.

55.002 was already in pristine two-tone green livery and only needed its yellow front ends painting. 55.009 was rubbed down and totally repainted at York (commencing Sunday 11 October) and adorned with silver fuel tanks and a grey roof. 55.015 was out of service at Finsbury Park from 7 October, and was being prepared for the 'Wessex Deltic' tour (on 17 October). It was totally repainted and received its white cabs back; and was also treated at York between 19 and 21 October with grey roof sections and silver fuel tanks; it still carried its white cabs for a short while until they were painted out later at York. No 55.015 only worked four service trains and one 'Deltic' tour in

this condition, these being the 08.50 York-Liverpool, 13.05 Liverpool-York, 15.50 York-Liverpool and 20.40 Liverpool-York on test on the 22 October, and then the York -Aberdeen 'Deltic Salute' on 24 October. 55.015 had its white cabs painted out by 3 November.

55.022 had been out of service at Stratford Traction Repair Shops since 9 September for collision damage repairs after colliding with 55.021 at Finsbury Park. It was decided that 'Deltic' No 22 was to be prepared at Stratford with silver fuel tanks and grey roof sections as 55.009 and 55.015 were to have. Authority was also given for the number 'D9000' to be painted at the opposite end to the '55.022'.

Instructions were issued that the four nominated 'Deltics' were to be kept inside York depot and not to be used for general traffic, except trial runs prior to working a special; the usual trial run was the 08.50 York-Liverpool and the 13.05 Liverpool-York, or the 08.07 York-Kings Cross and the 16.03 Kings Cross-York. Despite these instructions the four nominated 'Deltics' were often found working in traffic for several days after working a special because of the shortage of motive power.

On Thursday 8 October, whilst working the 22.15 Kings Cross-Aberdeen train, 55.008 had trouble with number one engine in the Thirsk area, and was removed at Newcastle in the early hours of the morning and sent to Gateshead depot for inspection. It was discovered that number one power-unit auxiliary generator drive had sheared, and so 55.008 was sent light engine to York in the afternoon of the same day. The repair was one which could be normally made at its home depot, but, not only had the auxiliary generator drive sheared, it had also damaged the main generator air manifold cooling system. Hence the

Below:
55.018 and 55.002 inside York depot on 14 October 1981. *D. B. Stacey*

locomotive's number one power-unit was isolated and 55.008 was restricted to one engine.

On Saturday 10 October 55.002 worked the 'Two Firths Express' Railtour from York to Edinburgh and return. Every Saturday following this special until the 'Deltics' were withdrawn from service (except Saturday 26 December) saw at least one 'Deltic' working a special.

Sunday 11 October found 55.018 working what were to be its last Anglo-Scottish trains, the 11.25 Edinburgh-Plymouth, 09.00 Plymouth-Edinburgh (to and from York), then finally southbound to London on the 21.20 Aberdeen-Kings Cross (sleepers only, which was formed of dual-heated stock). Early Monday morning on its journey south, number one engine was cutting out intermittently. After arrival at Kings Cross the locomotive went to Finsbury Park where it was fuelled and examined to determine why the engine was shutting down. Finsbury Park found that number one engine was aerating, which meant that another power-unit was required, and York depot was informed of the current state of 55.018. Once again there were three 'Deltics' restricted to one engine – 55.008, 55.011 and 55.018. That morning a decision had to be made to withdraw either 55.008 or 55.018, so that one 'Deltic' could have the other's good power-unit, hence making one good locomotive. The Traction Maintenance Engineer at York was asked to

make the decision: the axe fell on 55.018 because its boiler was isolated, and 55.008 was favoured because it was dual heat, both electric and steam train heat systems being operative. It was intended that 55.018 would be towed dead to York for cannibalisation before the power-unit change was to be carried out. However, because of the shortage of motive power at Kings Cross, it was allowed one more journey, this being the 19.40 Kings Cross-Hull, restricted to one engine. Whilst at Retford the driver requested a fresh locomotive at Doncaster because 55.018 was having trouble maintaining its air pressure. On arrival at Doncaster *Ballymoss* was removed from the train, and ran light to York under its own power for the last time, arriving shortly after midnight. The fault was

Above left:
55.013 hands over to 50.033 at York on 16 October on the 09.50 Edinburgh-Plymouth train. *D. B. Stacey*

Left:
17 October was a busy day for 'Deltics' with no less than three specials. Here we see the 'Wessex Deltic' railtour at Bournemouth headed by 55.015, ready to depart for Eastleigh and Portsmouth Harbour. *J. Chalcraft*

Top:
55.021 departs York in style with the Honiton Round Table's 'Minsterman' railtour to Scarborough. *D. B. Stacey*

Above:
The third railtour on 17 October: 55.009 at Burntisland with a special from Newcastle. *A. J. McLean*

diagnosed to be number two straight air brake valve blowing through. This was not repaired because the locomotive was taken out of service on arrival at York and cannibalised for spares.

On 13 October 55.022 was released at Stratford after a lengthy stay and travelled light engine to Finsbury Park. Leaving the depot the following morning to work the 09.40 Kings Cross-York train, 55.022 was derailed and sustained traction motor gearcase and brake gear damage.

55.008 and 55.011, both restricted to one engine, became regular visitors to Liverpool, usually on the 08.50 and 15.50 from York returning with the 13.05 and 20.40 from Liverpool.

On Thursday 15 October 55.007 worked the 08.07 York-Kings Cross train, but arrived on one engine. At Finsbury Park it was discovered that number two power-unit had a fractured cylinder liner and a restriction of one engine was placed on *Pinza*, thus putting the 'Deltic' fleet back to having three working on one engine.

55.002 was given a trial run out to Liverpool with the 08.50 from York on Friday 16 October, the first of many trial runs on this train for the four nominated 'Deltics'. The engine was required at Gateshead to work a Newcastle-Inverness special the next day. Returning from Liverpool on the 14.05 Newcastle train, it was found to be down on power and was unable to obtain more than 70mph, but even so it went through to Newcastle where it was stopped for repairs at Gateshead. With three 'Deltics' required for specials the next day, Saturday 17 October, the situation was getting serious. 55.022 had been the original choice to work the 'Wessex Deltic' railtour but was still out of service at Finsbury Park after being derailed, and so 55.015 was chosen to work this special. 55.009 was earmarked to work a Plymouth-Scarborough special forward from York. By the afternoon of 16 October, 55.021 had emerged from Doncaster Works and run light to Finsbury Park to work the 19.40 Kings Cross-Hull train and empty stock to York. It was decided to send 55.009 to Newcastle for the Inverness special and use 55.021, albeit rather filthy, for the Scarborough train. 55.009 worked the 20.00 Kings Cross-Aberdeen train from York to Newcastle for this purpose. The following day the three specials were worked by their final booked 'Deltics', 55.009 working from Newcastle to Perth, light engine to Aberdeen, and returning with the special to Newcastle, and 55.015 visiting Bournemouth, Eastleigh and Portsmouth Harbour.

Sunday 18 October was 55.018's official withdrawal date after being taken out of traffic at York the previous Monday to be cannibalised, bringing the 'Deltic' fleet down to 15 locomotives. 55.009 and 55.015 returned to York Depot to join 55.002 which had run light engine from Gateshead the previous day; the fourth 'nominated' 'Deltic', 55.022, was still under repair at Finsbury Park.

The following day 55.016, which had been stopped for repairs at Finsbury Park since 12 October, was restricted to one engine as number two power-unit's radiator fan cardan shaft was adrift and camshaft damaged. 55.016 was also robbed of brake equipment for 55.022 and did not return to traffic until 20 October, working the 01.00 Kings Cross-Newcastle train restricted to one engine.

On Tuesday 20 October 55.018 was towed to Stratford from York in the company of 40.068, dragged by 31.406, ready to have its good power-unit installed in 55.008. The same day 55.002 visited Liverpool for a trial run on the 08.50 York-Liverpool and the 13.05 Liverpool-York, followed by 55.015 two days later which also worked the 15.50 York-Liverpool and the 20.40 Liverpool-York, in preparation for the 'Deltic Salute' railtour the following Saturday.

During the week there had been a change of mind as to which 'Deltic' was to receive 55.018's power-unit. Instead of the originally chosen 55.008 it was now to be 55.007, which was towed from York to Stratford on the 23rd for the power-unit change.

This was to be the first of many engine changes performed at Stratford Traction Repair Shops, and the first time that a power-unit change had been performed

Below:
A more conventional working on 17 October was 55.004 heading the 09.50 Edinburgh-Plymouth train, seen here at Skelton Junction. *C. J. Tuffs*

Right:
55.015 passing Diggle on 22 October with the 13.05 Liverpool-York service. *Tulyar* made two Trans-Pennine outings on this particular day. *G. W. Morrison*

away from Doncaster Works since it had taken over responsibility for engine maintenance from English Electric.

On Saturday 24 October 55.015 worked the 'Deltic' Preservation Society's 'Deltic Salute' railtour from York to Aberdeen and back. Later that evening 55.021 worked a very unusual train, a 9Z11 21.13 Crofton-Gascoigne Wood long welded rail train. On 27 October 55.021 worked the 22.08 York-Shrewsbury mail train as far as Stockport and back to York on the 22.50 Shrewsbury-York mail train. This had now become a very rare working, but there was to be one more visit to Stockport in December. That same evening 55.004, working the 23.30 Hull-Clifton Carriage Sidings empty coaching stock off the 19.40 Kings Cross-Hull train, lost power on an engine between Doncaster and York. In the early hours of the next morning it was found that number two power-unit was de-phased and 55.004 was restricted to one engine. It was allocated to the 07.49 York-Liverpool and the 12.05 return on 28 October, whilst 55.011 was placed on the 08.50 York-Liverpool and 13.05 return to York. During the day it was decided in view of the number of 'Deltics' restricted to one engine (now totalling four) to withdraw 55.004 to provide a good power unit for 55.008. 55.004 was turned round at

Above:
An immaculate 55.015 *Tulyar* arrives at Newcastle Central on 24 October 1981 with the 'Deltic Salute' railtour. The wreath donated by the Yorkshire branch of the 'Deltic' Preservation Society was to make several appearances during the 'Deltics' last months.
P. M. Marsh

Below:
The four 'nominated' 'Deltics' were to be found inside York depot on the evening of 27 October, together with 55.008. *C. W. Fellows*

York to work the 15.50 York-Liverpool train, but at Manchester it was suffering high water temperature, and at Liverpool the red fault light showed up. It was decided not to risk using 55.004 for the 20.40 Liverpool-York train, and so it was arranged that it would be double-headed back to York on the 20.40 with 55.011 which was due to arrive on the 15.18 from Newcastle (having re-engined the train at York).

Above:
55.004 stands at York on 28 October ready to work its last train, the 15.50 to Liverpool. *P. J. Chambers*

Below:
The end for 55.004: 55.011, restricted to one engine, couples up ready to pull 55.004 with the 20.40 Liverpool-York, but the driver later decided not to have a fuel-laden locomotive in tow. *P. J. Chambers*

55.011 was coupled up with 55.004 and ran to the platform end, but at this point the driver apparently had a change of mind and decided he was not going to drag 55.004 in the train because of the amount of fuel it was carrying. Therefore 55.004 was stabled at Liverpool for the night, already sentenced to withdrawal. Next morning, 29 October, 55.002 was given a run out to Liverpool on the usual 08.50 from York in preparation for the 'Celtic Deltic' railtour on Saturday 31 October. 31.405 was sent to Liverpool to tow 55.004 back to York.

55.017 arrived on York shed shortly after midnight on 30 October with only one engine running having worked the 19.40 Kings Cross-Hull and the 23.30 Hull-Clifton Carriage Sidings empty stock. It was found that number one engine was de-phased, so yet another 'Deltic' was restricted to one engine, joining 55.008, 55.011 and 55.016. 55.004 was towed to Stratford in the company of 47.019 and 47.411 the same day, ready to give its good power-unit to 55.008; that same day 55.007 emerged from Stratford after a power-unit change with withdrawn 55.018.

Friday 30 October also saw the last 'Deltic' working on the 09.50 Edinburgh-Plymouth and the 07.36 Plymouth-Edinburgh trains north of York – 55.021 was the locomotive in both directions. The northbound service switched to a High Speed Train on Sunday 1 November and the southbound service the next day. An amendment was issued to the locomotive programme, as follows.

TRAIN WORKING	ARR	DEP	WTT NO	DAYS RUN
No 3				
Off 2				
Class 55				
Haymarket depot		19.50	0E35	SX
Edinburgh (SH)	19.57	20.25	1E35	
Kings Cross	04.45	05.25	0B02	MX
Fin Park depot	05.45			
FUEL				
Works 4				
No 3				
Off 2				
Class 55				
Spare, Haymarket depot				SO
Works 3				
No 3				
Off 3				
Class 55				
Spare, Haymarket depot				SUO
Works 4				

Below left:
55.002 approaches Marsden on 29 October with the 13.05 Liverpool-York train. *G.W. Morrison*

Above:
The British Rail-organised 'Celtic Deltic' railtour headed by 55.002 passes through Selby on 31 October.
P. M. Marsh

Below:
45.005 towing 55.022 to York depot on 4 November after working the 13.05 train from Liverpool; on the right 55.017 runs light engine from York to Peterborough.
C. W. Fellows

On Saturday 31 October 55.002 worked the 'Celtic Deltic' railtour from Kings Cross to Edinburgh and back to Peterborough. That same day an unusual push-pull working occurred when 55.010 working the 15.50 York-Kings Cross failed between Gasworks and Copenhagen tunnels outside Kings Cross with a brake defect. 55.011 was summoned from Finsbury Park to push the train the short distance to Kings Cross.

55.004 was condemned officially on 1 November, bringing the 'Deltic' fleet down to 14. 55.008 ran light engine from Finsbury Park to Stratford to have 55.004's good power unit installed, and one of the other 'Deltics' restricted to 'one engine', 55.016, was

able to be repaired at York depot having a traction motor blower fitted from withdrawn 55.018: it was released back into traffic on two engines on 2 November, working the 08.07 York-Kings Cross on the 3rd. This just left 55.011 and 55.017 needing power-units, although 55.011 was earmarked for the last reconditioned power-unit still being prepared at Doncaster Works. The next day, 4 November, 55.022 was given a trial run out to Liverpool, once again on the 08.50 from York, but shortly after pulling out of Liverpool with the 13.05 return working it suffered a double flashover, with number one engine's main generator catching fire. It reached Manchester Victoria where assistance in the shape of 45.005 was at hand, and this towed the train through to York. On examination at York depot it was found that number one power-unit generator was unable to be repaired and thus another engine was required. The Traction Maintenance Engineer at York depot expressed his concern over the general unreliability of 55.022 and suggested that another 'Deltic', either 55.007 or 55.013, take its place to work specials. 55.022 was taken out of traffic pending a decision on its future. Meanwhile 55.015 had worked the 08.07 York-Kings Cross and 16.03 return as a trial run for Saturday's 'Deltic Queen of Scots' railtour. Two 'Deltics' were needed for this special because of the short turn-round time at Edinburgh – 55.015 to work north and 55.022 to work south, but with 55.022 awaiting decision 55.002 had to be chosen in its place.

Above:
The weather could not have been better for the official line-up of 'Deltics' on 5 November, with clear blue skies and brilliant sunshine. Here 55.015 and 55.022 give a menacing appearance during the line-up at York.
P. E. Gash

Below:
T&N Railtours organised the 'Deltic Queen of Scots' railtour from London to Edinburgh via Leeds, Hartlepool and Sunderland on 7 November. This is 55.015 *Tulyar*, now minus its white cabs, pausing at Leeds where a party of children from St Christopher's orphanage joined the train. *P. M. Marsh*

Above:
55.002 at Carlisle on 9 November with the 15.53 to Edinburgh. *P. E. Gash*

Left:
37.082 assisting 55.014 at Morpeth on 10 November with the 08.10 Newcastle-Edinburgh service – this was 'The Duke's' last train. *K. Morton*

The next day, 5 November, all the nominated 'Deltics' – 55.002, 55.009, 55.015 and 55.022 – had been collected at York depot and were lined up for a photographic session by a British Rail photographer. During the same day it was decided to keep 55.022 running, and because 55.011's reconditioned power-unit still wasn't ready at Doncaster Works, it was decided to withdraw 55.011 to provide a good power-unit for 55.022. 55.011 was at Haymarket on 5 November and worked the 17.07 Edinburgh-Newcastle stopping train and its last train, the 22.55 Newcastle-Kings Cross service. It was an unfortunate ending for 55.011, which had run on one engine since

30 September and given very little trouble on its Trans-Pennine and overnight East Coast main line trains. After arriving at Kings Cross on 6 November, 55.011 went to Finsbury Park and from there to Stratford. Later that day 55.022 ran light diesel from York to Stratford for the power-unit change with 55.011 – so by now there were no less than five 'Deltics' at Stratford: 55.018 condemned, 55.008 having 55.004's good power-unit installed, and 55.022 having 55.011's good engine fitted. 55.002 worked the 15.50 York-Kings Cross and 22.15 Kings Cross-Edinburgh trains to enable the locomotive to be in position ready for the special the next day, whilst 55.015 ran light from York to Finsbury Park to work the first leg of the 'Deltic Queen of Scots' railtour from Kings Cross to Edinburgh.

On Sunday 8 November 55.011 was officially withdrawn, bringing the 'Deltic' fleet down to 13. Two days later, on the 10th, 55.014 failed with complete

17

loss of power at Cramlington, when working the 08.10 Newcastle-Edinburgh train. It was not known at the time, but this was to be its last train. 37.082 assisted the train forward to Edinburgh, where 55.014 was towed to Haymarket for examination. There it was found that number one traction motor needed renewing and number two motor had water contamination. In the evening 55.019 was released from Doncaster Works;

Left:
55.007 *Pinza* at Kings Cross on 13 November after working the 20.25 Edinburgh-Kings Cross train.
K. Alison

Below left:
55.017 leaves Doncaster Works on 18 November after receiving the last reconditioned power-unit for the 'Deltic' fleet. This was the last repair carried out by the works on the Class 55s while they were in service.
A. Whitehouse

Below:
Another failure for 55.022: looking immaculate at Leeds on 20 November, it had just been removed from the 08.50 York-Liverpool train. *C. W. Fellows*

Above right:
55.002 waits to depart Leeds on 21 November with the RCTS and British Rail 'Deltic Scotsman' railtour.
P. M. Marsh

Right:
55.013 pauses at Doncaster on a cold 24 November evening with the 20.19 York-Kings Cross train.
P. M. Marsh

Below right:
An unusual view of 55.009 *Alycidon* at Liverpool Lime Street on 25 November with the 13.05 to York.
C. W. Fellows

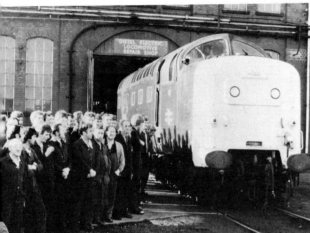

running light engine to Peterborough it was intercepted at Ponton (near Grantham) to assist 6C30, the 13.55 Tyneside Central Freight Depot-Dagenham Dock train which had failed. It assisted the train to Peterborough, and then worked the 22.15 Kings Cross-Aberdeen train, which had also failed, forward to Edinburgh.

The following day 55.014 was towed from Haymarket to Gateshead by 47.710, and from there to York where it was to wait for a traction motor from 55.004 which was still in Stratford. 55.008 and 55.022 were released from Stratford on 12 November leaving 55.004, 55.011 and 55.018 all condemned with six power-units unserviceable. 55.009 was given a run out to Liverpool on 12 November with the 08.50 York-Liverpool, and returned on the 13.05 Liverpool-York train, and 55.017 travelled light to Doncaster Works to have the last reconditioned power-unit fitted, the one originally intended for

55.011. For the first time in many weeks not one 'Deltic' had a restriction of one engine. Two days later, on the 14th, 55.009 worked the 'Deltic Cumbrian' railtour, traversing the Settle & Carlisle line.

55.004 could not be moved from Stratford to York because of a shortage of resources, so 55.014 was left at York waiting for a traction motor. On Tuesday 17 November the CM&EE at York decided to withdraw 55.014 to provide parts for other 'Deltics'. 55.002 was chosen to work the 'Deltic Scotsman' railtour the following Saturday, the 21st and once again visited Liverpool on the 18th. Later the same day 55.017 was released from Doncaster Works amid great ceremony, this being the final repair carried out on the 'Deltics' while they were in service.

An unplanned 'Deltic' visit to Liverpool occurred

the next day when 55.002 was pressed into service to work the 15.50 train from York, no other locomotive being available. 55.022 had another unsuccessful outing the next morning; placed on the 08.50 York-Liverpool train it lost an engine at Holgate Junction, just a few hundred yards from York station. It struggled on to Leeds, whistling off for a fresh engine while passing Peckfield signalbox. At Leeds 55.022 was detached and later returned to York depot, there it was found that number one power-unit had shut down because of the fuel racks jamming.

On Saturday 21 November 55.002 worked the 'Deltic Scotsman' railtour from York to Inverkeithing via the Settle & Carlisle line and Newcastle. Arrival at Edinburgh was about 80 minutes late, due mainly to 55.002 slipping very badly leaving Carlisle. As the locomotive required fuel and water 55.013 was placed

on the train to Bradford and York. The same day 55.021 covered for an HST failure by working the 12.15 Edinburgh-Kings Cross train as far as Newcastle. 55.002 returned south with the 22.30 Edinburgh-Kings Cross train, but when coming off Finsbury Park depot the next morning to work the 10.05 Kings Cross-York Sunday service, a con-rod broke and went through the 'B' and 'C' banks of number two engine, so another power-unit was required. Sunday 22 November was also 55.014's official withdrawal date, bringing the 'Deltic' fleet down to 12.

Early Monday morning, the 23rd, 55.004, 55.011 and 55.018 were towed away from Stratford by 31.324 on a 9G36 01.23 Stratford to Doncaster and York special freight. This unusual procession of three dead 'Deltics' travelled via Cambridge, March and Lincoln to Doncaster. During a stop-over at Lincoln 31.281 took over from 31.324 to haul the locomotives to Decoy yard at Doncaster. It was the intention to detach 55.011 and 55.018 and bring 55.004 through to York, but because of crewing difficulties all three locomotives went through, arriving at York shortly after midnight on 24 November. 55.004 was detached, and 55.011 and 55.018 were taken back to Doncaster and placed in the works complex shortly after arrival.

While the three condemned 'Deltics' were being towed down on the 23rd, 55.021 worked the Trade Union Congress-sponsored 'Jobs Express' charter train from Edinburgh to Glasgow Central and returned light to Haymarket, a very rare working. 55.002 returned to York early Tuesday morning after it had worked north on the Sunday's 22.30 Kings Cross-Edinburgh train, south on the Monday with the 17.06 Edinburgh-Newcastle, then around the coast from Newcastle to Darlington with the 21.20 Newcastle-Darlington and Kings Cross sleepers, and light engine to York, all on one engine. It was decided to install one of 55.014's good power units in 55.002, and for this reason 55.002 towed 40.058 and 55.014 to Stratford later that morning.

Three 'Deltic'-hauled specials were planned for the forthcoming Saturday: 55.022 was specifically requested for the 'Deltic Venturer' York to Paddington special, 55.009 was chosen to work a Newcastle-Carlisle-Edinburgh railtour, and 55.015 was nominated for the 'Deltic Devonian' excursion, providing it was available, having been on repairs since 21 November with a brake failure at Finsbury Park. 55.009 went to Liverpool on 25 November, and 55.022 made its second outing of the week the next day (having gone on the Monday) 23 November. 55.017 was restricted to 'electric train heat only' on 25 November, its boiler water tank being holed and the 'flexible' on the main steam pipe missing. By Thursday it was becoming clear that 55.015 was not going to be available for the Saturday, which left 55.002 as the only alternative; fortunately the latter was released from Stratford after a power-unit change with 55.014. It was given a trial run out the next day

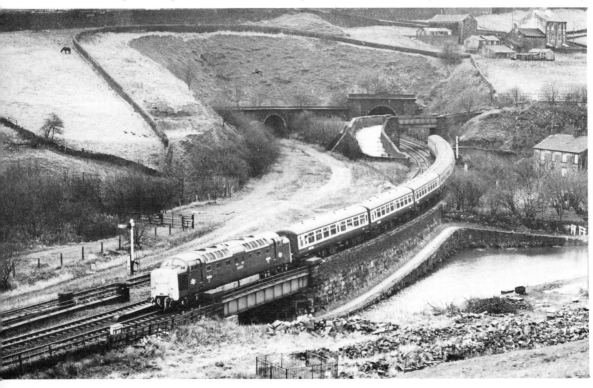

Above:
55.008 and 55.017 stand in the fuelling bay at York depot in the early hours of 4 December. Both 'Deltics' had by this time been restricted to electric train heating only.
P. E. Gash

Below left:
55.009 leaving Standedge Tunnel on 3 December with the 13.05 Liverpool-York train. *G. W. Morrison*

Below:
The 'Hadrian Flyer' railtour on 5 December, headed by 55.015, crossing Ribblehead viaduct. *Tulyar* was the last 'Deltic' over the Settle & Carlisle line. *J. Matthews*

(the 27th) on the 09.40 Kings Cross-York and 14.15 return, and given the 'ok' for the special. However, the following morning 55.002's number two power-unit's main generator was found to be down to earth and 55.002 was once again restricted to one engine and therefore unable to work the 'Deltic Devonian'. 55.016, which had worked the 20.25 Edinburgh-Kings Cross train, was hastily placed on the 'Deltic Devonian' special to Exeter. Meanwhile, 55.022 worked the 'Deltic Venturer' railtour from York to Paddington. Hundreds of people turned out to see this particular special, with Birmingham New Street in particular a mass of enthusiasts. The highlight of the special was the climb up Lickey incline just north of Bromsgrove, with a speed restriction of 20mph at the bottom of the incline and a load of 11 coaches. Nevertheless, *Royal Scots Grey* accelerated up the slope to reach 30mph at the top, a truly remarkable feat. On the same day 55.009 visited Carlisle and Edinburgh with a special from Newcastle.

55.002 was called to Stratford three days later, on Tuesday 2 December, to have 55.014's other good power unit installed. 55.008, undergoing a 'C' exam at York, had its boiler isolated on 1 December because of burst element tubes, and joined 55.017 in being restricted to electric train heating only. 55.015 was chosen to work the next railtour on the forthcoming Saturday and visited Liverpool twice the next day, 2 December, on the 08.50 and 15.50 trains from York, no other locomotive being available for the latter train.

Above:
55.015 stands at the familiar platform nine at York on 10 December with the 20.00 Kings Cross-Aberdeen train. Later that night it was to suffer a serious fire at Leuchars. *K. Alison*

Right:
Illuminated by station lights at York on 12 December, 55.002 waits with the return special to Norwich. *D. Cooper*

55.017 made a rare visit to Polmadie in Glasgow the same day, working an empty van train from Craigentinny. 55.009 made a Liverpool trip on Thursday, followed there by 55.022 on Friday. 55.002 returned from Stratford to Finsbury Park on 4 December, having had the last power unit change performed on a 'Deltic' in service. 55.014, now with two defective power-units from 55.002, was towed to Doncaster Works by 37.004 early on the Saturday morning. 55.004 remained at York to provide spares.

55.015 worked 'The Hadrian Flyer' railtour from Peterborough to Carlisle and Newcastle on 5 December, once again traversing the Settle & Carlisle line, the last time a 'Deltic' used this route. 55.007 *Pinza* worked the 15.50 York-Liverpool and 20.40 return, making a change from the nominated 'Deltics'.

Three days later on 8 December, 55.021, working the 20.00 Kings Cross-Aberdeen train, failed at York with loss of coolant. This was diagnosed the following day as number two power-unit aerating, and a 'one engine' restriction was placed on the locomotive – a restriction which stayed with 55.021 until withdrawal. The next morning 55.022 made a what was by now rare visit to Kings Cross with the 08.07 from York, in order to gain press coverage in the locomotives' final weeks of operation.

At 06.30 the following day, the 10th, all 12 'Deltics' left in service were available for traffic, with just 55.021 restricted to one engine. 55.009 was chosen to work BR Scottish Region's farewell 'Deltic' special the coming weekend and once again visited Liverpool, and 55.002 was selected for a Norwich-York railtour. 55.015 didn't return to York after working 'The Hadrian Flyer', finding itself in general traffic because of a shortage of motive power. Early on Friday morning, the 11th, it was working the 22.15 Kings Cross-Aberdeen train forward from Edinburgh when number two engine caught fire at Leuchars. The locomotive was removed from the train and returned to Haymarket where examination found that the power-unit had exhaust, silencer and lagging fire damage.

In the early hours of Saturday 12 December, 55.010, working the 22.55 Newcastle-Kings Cross train, failed at Doncaster after losing a power-unit. The failure was diagnosed as number two power-unit aerating, so 55.010 joined 55.021 in being restricted to one engine. 55.009 worked the 'Grampian Deltic'

railtour from Edinburgh to Aberdeen via Perth and 55.002 headed a Norwich-York special after going light from Peterborough to work the train. The proposed 'Tees-Tyne Pullman' special from Carlisle to Kings Cross via Newcastle had to be cancelled because British Rail was unable to guarantee a 'Deltic'. 55.007 visited Liverpool for the second successive Saturday with the 15.18 train from Newcastle, having previously substituted for an HST failure by working the 09.15 Edinburgh-Kings Cross train as far as Newcastle. In the evening 55.019, working the 20.00 Kings Cross-Aberdeen train, failed at Peterborough after freezing up in the bitter cold weather that was affecting the country at the time. Number one engine's

Above:
A fine evening study of 55.007 *Pinza* at York on 12 December in charge of the 15.18 Newcastle-Liverpool service. *D. Cooper*

Below:
During the same evening 55.016 is seen at Doncaster at the head of a more conventional train, the 18.14 York-Kings Cross. *D. Cooper*

oil radiator was leaking because of a burst element and so yet another 'Deltic' was restricted to one engine.

The following day 55.010 made a rare Sunday visit to Liverpool on the 15.40 from York. 55.002 remained

at Norwich and wasn't moved until 15 December because no crews were available to fetch it. 55.010 made a repeat trip to Liverpool on Monday 14 December, with the 08.50 from York, while 55.009 substituted for an HST failure by working the 10.25 Aberdeen-Kings Cross train from Edinburgh to York. On Tuesday 55.015 was towed from Haymarket to York by 47.522; there it had a silencer and roof section off 55.004 fitted to replace those damaged in the fire at Leuchars. 55.017 took a trial run of Mk III sleepers from Edinburgh to Aberdeen, although officially 'Deltics' were barred from working this new stock: this is believed to be the only time a 'Deltic' in fact worked Mk III sleepers. 55.009 *Alycidon* made the last 'Deltic' visit to Carlisle with the 07.18 train from Edinburgh and the 15.53 return on 15 December. Later that day 55.013 arrived at Finsbury Park after working the 14.15 York-Kings Cross train with a coolant leak on number two engine. Examination found a split header tank and radiator fan clutch slipping, so another 'Deltic' was restricted to one engine.

The bitter cold weather began to take its toll on locomotives, particularly on overnight services, and 'Deltics' were no exception. Early Wednesday morning on 16 December, 55.007, working the 23.20 Kings Cross-Aberdeen train, failed at Newcastle with its brakes frozen and was taken to Gateshead for repairs. Soon after, 55.019 on the 00.05 Kings

Cross-Newcastle train failed at Aycliffe, Co-Durham with loss of air and was assisted to Newcastle by 45.076. The third 'Deltic' failure of the day proved to be significant. 55.013, restricted to one engine, was allocated to the 07.23 Peterborough-Kings Cross service, subsequently its last train. The 'Deltic' failed at Wood Green with number one engine shutting down, so 31.292 assisted the train forward to Kings Cross. Diagnosis at Finsbury Park showed the problem to be a fractured liner, so now both power-units were out of service: 55.013 didn't work again.

55.019 failed for the second time that day when working the 21.00 Newcastle-Kings Cross service, being taken off the train at Doncaster because of a defective compressor governor. 55.021 reached Bradford Exchange early on 17 December by working the 23.00 Kings Cross-Bradford train ('Deltics' were now very rare visitors to this city). Four more 'Deltic' failures occurred that day, making eight in two days. The first of these was 55.002 at York on the 20.35 Aberdeen-Kings Cross train with number two engine cutting out because the overspeed tripped. 55.016, which had just come off a 'B' exam and boiler repairs at York, re-engined the train, but the driver stopped at Chaloners Whin to request a fresh engine at Doncaster because of boiler failure. However, 55.016 only got as far as Daw Lane crossing (just north of Doncaster) before failing with an AWS horn defect and the compressors not running. 08.115 dragged the 'Deltic' and train into Doncaster where 55.016 was taken to the depot. The third failure was 55.008 on the 08.07 York-Kings Cross train, which was terminated at Peterborough because the 'Deltic's' brakes froze. The fourth casualty occurred much later in the day when

Below:
55.022 heads through the snow near Salford on 17 December with the 13.05 Liverpool-York train.
G. W. Morrison

55.021, working the 21.20 Bradford-Kings Cross train from Leeds, failed at Wakefield because of an exhaust manifold defect. 25.083 assisted the train forward to Doncaster where the 'Deltic' was removed. During the day 55.022 had made a trip to Liverpool, and 55.007 had come off repairs at Gateshead still restricted to one engine as number one power-unit's fuel pump wasn't working. Thus by the evening of 17 December no less than five of the remaining 12 'Deltics' left in service were restricted to one engine – Nos 7, 10, 13, 19 and 21. 55.010 made the last Deltic visit to Stockport that night, working the 22.08 York-Shrewsbury train.

The following morning 55.009, in charge of the 20.25 Edinburgh-Kings Cross train, failed at Doncaster with its brake cylinder gauges frozen up, while heading for London to be prepared for the

Above left:
The other railtour on 19 December, the 'Napier North-Eastern', also had heating problems because 55.002's boiler didn't work. Here we see the locomotive at Scarborough. *G. Scott-Lowe*

Above:
55.017 stands on the blocks at Kings Cross on 19 December, having worked a 12.25 additional from Edinburgh. *L. Braithwaite*

Below:
The 'Deltic Broadsman' railtour on 19 December headed by 55.009, at Norwich. This was the worst-run railtour of the last months, with guard problems, one coach short, heating problems and very late running (the Lowestoft section had to be missed out). *C. W. Fellows*

'Deltic Broadsman' railtour the next day (55.002 had been the original choice but had failed at York on the 17th). Fortunately it was possible to thaw out 55.009, which ran light to Finsbury Park before working the special the next day. 55.015 and 55.022 were on repairs at York so 55.002, with its boiler not working, had to work the 'Napier North Eastern' railtour from Plymouth forward from York to Scarborough, Bridlington and Doncaster.

Sunday 20 December saw two 'Deltic' visits to Liverpool – the Leeds Divisional Passenger Office had seen the potential of using 'Deltics' on Liverpool services drawing many enthusiasts to travel behind them. The 15.40 York-Liverpool and 19.10 return services were advertised as being 'Deltic'-hauled; because of turn-round difficulties at Liverpool, the 09.45 from Edinburgh to Liverpool also had to be 'Deltic'-hauled. 55.022 took the latter train forward from York, running via Bradford and Halifax complete with a 'Trans-Pennine Deltic Lament' headboard, and 55.002 followed on the advertised 15.40 York-Liverpool train. At Liverpool 55.022 was placed on the 19.10 York service and 55.002 returned with the 21.15 train. Also on this date 55.013 was officially withdrawn: now the 'Deltic' fleet stood at 11.

55.016, now restricted to 'electric train heat only', worked the 08.07 York-Kings Cross train the following day, 21 December, but was removed from the train at Peterborough after suffering a severe collector drum fire on number one engine. 55.010 ran light from York heading for Kings Cross but failed at Peterborough because oil was coming from the silencer of number one power-unit. 55.007 was released back into traffic, once again on two engines. Next morning, the 22nd, 55.016 towed 55.010 from Peterborough to Doncaster, both going there for repairs. They were released the following day (23 December) and ran light

to Finsbury Park, their last visit to the capital. 55.016 was then allocated to the 19.40 Kings Cross-Hull, and 55.010 to the 23.00 Kings Cross-Bradford train. After arriving at Hull, 55.016 worked the 23.30 stock to Clifton, which was its last train because at York it was stopped for repairs after number one engine shut down. The locomotive was put on an 'A' exam and needed to

be reblocked. A build up of oil in the collector drum of number one power-unit was discovered, indicating a leakage, and because another power-unit would probably be needed and its boiler was isolated, 55.016 was not released back into traffic.

Meanwhile, on the 23.00 Kings Cross-Bradford train, 55.010 failed at Corby Glen with a fractured lubricating oil pipe on number one engine. The train was assisted in the rear by 47.458 (working the 23.55 Kings Cross-Aberdeen service) as far as Grantham. 55.019 was started up at Doncaster depot but failed shortly after coming off shed with frozen brakes, and so 37.137 was despatched from Doncaster Carr locoshed to run light to Grantham and hauled 55.010 plus train to Doncaster, where the 'Deltic' was taken to the depot. With both power-units now out of use

55.010 was officially withdrawn the same day (Christmas Eve) and 55.019 took it the short journey across to the Works. Ten 'Deltics' now remained.

Christmas Eve saw a fair amount of 'Deltic' activity: besides 55.010 failing, 55.021 worked the 00.05 Kings Cross-Newcastle, 55.017 the 05.50 Kings Cross-Aberdeen throughout and the 16.30 return to York, 55.009 the 08.50 York-Liverpool and 13.05 return, and 55.008 made a surprising trip to Glasgow (being the last 'Deltic' to visit the city) on the 18.00 from Edinburgh, returning with the 19.30, and 55.019 worked the 18.14 York-Kings Cross train, but failed at Doncaster.

The first 'Deltic' to turn a wheel after the Christmas break was 55.007 *Pinza* on the 10.05 Kings Cross-York train on 27 December. After only a short distance one engine was lost; at York it was found that number one power-unit had cut out with low coolant, so it was topped up and tested but no visible leaks were seen. It returned to London on the 19.10 from York. 55.009 and 55.015 made the Trans-Pennine trip to Liverpool, repeating the previous Sunday's workings, and a large crowd gathered at Lime Street to see what was thought by many to be the last 'Deltic' visit there. 55.009 departed with the 19.10 to York and 55.015 with the 21.15. The following day 55.007, working the 09.40 Kings Cross-York train, again lost an engine en route and was stopped for repairs on arrival at York. Apparently number one power-unit was again losing coolant, but still no leaks were found.

55.009 was chosen to work the 'Deltic Executive' special the next day but saw considerable activity

Below:
The 'Deltic Executive' railtour of 29 December passing Cattal. *D. B. Stacey*

before reaching Finsbury Park on the evening of the 28th. 55.021 was also kept busy, working the 09.10 Dundee-Kings Cross train from Edinburgh, albeit on one engine.

On 29 December 55.009 *Alycidon* worked the last privately-chartered 'Deltic' special, the 'Deltic Executive', being the last 'Deltic' to visit Harrogate and Hull. 55.008 made the last 'Deltic' journey to Carstairs with the 09.07 train from Edinburgh, and the final visit to Aberdeen with the 14.55 from Edinburgh, returning on the 18.23 Aberdeen-Edinburgh. 55.021 soldiered on with one engine, again working the 09.10 Dundee-Kings Cross from Edinburgh, and 55.016 was officially withdrawn. Now only nine 'Deltics' remained.

The following day, Wednesday 30 December, was to see four 'Deltics' work their last trains. The first of these was 55.008 working overnight from Edinburgh with the 21.20 Aberdeen-Kings Cross train. On arrival at Finsbury Park it was taken out of service for a re-block, only a minor job, but *The Green Howards* never worked again. The second was 55.007: working the 08.07 York-Kings Cross train it got as far as Selby but then a fresh locomotive was requested at Doncaster because number one engine was cutting out and number two engine shutting down. It proceeded to Doncaster where 47.146 was attached to continue the journey to Kings Cross. At Finsbury Park it was found that number one power-unit was aerating and number two engine was losing coolant. The third 'Deltic' was 55.002. It was planned to use this 'Deltic' for the final special on Saturday 2 January 1982, along with 55.022. Therefore, the locomotive was allocated to the 07.49 York-Liverpool (the 08.50 being cancelled that

Above:
The 'Deltic Executive' of 29 December at Hull Paragon, 55.009 being the last 'Deltic' to visit the city.
C. W. Fellows

Below:
On 29 December 55.008 made the last 'Deltic' visits to Carstairs and Aberdeen. The photograph shows the locomotive at Aberdeen ready to depart for Edinburgh on the 18.23 service. *I. M. Flynn*

Right:
55.002 passes Earlestown on 30 December with the 12.05 Liverpool-York service. This was the locomotive's last train, and it was the last 'Deltic' to cross the Pennines. *E. Bellass*

Below right:
55.021's last visit to its original home depot, Haymarket, on 30 December. Gamely running on one engine to the bitter end, the locomotive clocked up an impressive mileage in its final week of service. *B. Roberton*

day) for a trial run, but number one engine kept shutting down because it was passing oil, and the overspeed was also tripping. At Liverpool it was decided the defect couldn't be repaired satisfactorily in time for the Saturday, and so it left Liverpool (the last 'Deltic' to do so) restricted to one engine, with its final run in BR service, the 12.05 Liverpool-York. On arrival at York it was taken up to the depot, and then later to the National Railway Museum annexe, a somewhat incongruous ending. Finally, 55.009 worked its last train. Having been taken off the 07.18 Edinburgh-Carlisle train at Newcastle due to boiler failure, it was repaired in time to work the 21.00

Newcastle-Kings Cross service. This, as it turned out, was its last train, as the locomotive was stopped for repairs at Finsbury Park because it required brake blocks and had a defective boiler.

Meanwhile, 55.017 had worked the 05.50 Kings Cross-Aberdeen train as far as Edinburgh, while 55.021 had again seen considerable activity working the 00.05 Kings Cross-Newcastle, the 08.10 Newcastle-Edinburgh and the 20.25 Edinburgh-Kings Cross trains. 55.019, after being out of action at Doncaster since Christmas Eve, ran light to London to work the 14.03 Kings Cross-York train, but then returned light engine back to the capital.

Because of 55.002's failure in traffic and 55.009's boiler problem, it was decided that 55.015 would work the outward leg of the final special, 55.022 the return leg, and 55.009 would act as standby. 55.022 would get to Edinburgh by working the 15.50 York-Kings Cross and 22.15 Kings Cross-Aberdeen trains on the 30th, and 55.015 would get to Finsbury Park by working the 15.50 York-Kings Cross train on the 31st. 55.009 would somehow get to York because the standby locomotive was booked to start from there. Unfortunately, the first part of the plan went wrong when 55.022 was stopped for repairs on arrival at Kings Cross because of a defective boiler and the number one cut-out switch contactor being burnt, and so 55.022 was unable to work north overnight.

The following day, Thursday 31 December, was the last day of 'Deltic' operation on ordinary service trains. 55.021 headed South overnight on the 20.25 Edinburgh-Kings Cross train, while 55.019 headed north on the 00.05 Kings Cross-Newcastle service. As dawn broke the plan was as follows:

● 55.022 to work the 05.50 Kings Cross-Aberdeen train as far as Edinburgh.
● 55.009 to work the 09.40 Kings Cross-York train and remain there ready to act as standby for Saturday's special.
● 55.008 to work the 14.03 Kings Cross-York train and be stored on arrival.
● 55.017 to work the 16.03 Kings Cross-York train and be stored on arrival.
● 55.021 to tow 55.007 and 55.013 to York for storage.
● 55.019 to return light engine from Newcastle to York after working the 00.05 Kings Cross-Newcastle train.

55.022 did work its booked train as far as Edinburgh where it was taken to Haymarket depot to wait for Saturday. 55.009 was not released off boiler repairs; it was found that several brake blocks were missing off 55.013 and brakes could not be obtained on the locomotive, so the plan to use 55.021 to tow 55.007 and 55.013 was abandoned, and in any case 55.021 was now needed to work the 09.40 Kings Cross-York train because it was a formation of steam heat stock. So, running on one engine, 55.021 left Kings Cross for the last time on its final train. On arrival at York it was taken to the depot for storing. 55.007 was towed from Finsbury Park to York by 31.121, leaving 55.013 behind. When the time came for 55.008 to be started up it was found to have flat batteries and had also been somewhat vandalised, and so *The Green Howards* remained at the Park.

55.015 *Tulyar* left York on the 15.50 train to Kings Cross as planned, and 55.017 had the honour of working the last 'Deltic' hauled service train out of

Kings Cross with the 16.03 departure to York, complete with headboard and wreath. However, on the Grantham side of Stoke tunnel the train was brought to a stand on signals – a broken rail had been found between Grantham and Newark, and single line working had been introduced. It was decided to terminate the 16.03 Kings Cross-York train at Grantham to ease congestion and line occupation, and use the locomotive and stock to run in the 15.50 York-Kings Cross train's path from Grantham as the latter train (with 55.015 at the head) had been heavily delayed south of Newark waiting a passage over the single line. Obviously this decision was not popular with the enthusiasts travelling behind 55.017, but realistically speaking, from an operational point of view, it was the correct decision to make. And so 55.017 was run-round at Grantham and headed south with a special '1G26' Grantham-Kings Cross train. However, leaving Grantham (at 18.58) and Stevenage, 55.017 suffered excessive wheelslip and came to a stand at milepost 28. WSR.5 (wheel slip relay No 5) was sticking, meaning the driver could only obtain

'tickover' power and not open the engine up fully. A wheelslip fault showed up on the instrument panel, and as neither the driver nor his secondman knew what the fault was, they decided to take the locomotive forward on tickover power, and the train crawled at a walking pace to milepost 28½, where the driver requested assistance. This came in the shape of 47.426 which pushed the train to Knebworth where it was terminated. Later 47.426 towed 55.017 and train empty stock to Kings Cross.

Meanwhile, at the other end of the country, 55.019 had continued north from Newcastle on the 08.10 train to Edinburgh, no other locomotive being available at Gateshead. It was thought it would return with the 17.18 train to Newcastle but in the event was allocated to the 16.30 Aberdeen-York train from Edinburgh. This was the last 'Deltic'-hauled service train, and the headboard and wreath were removed from 55.017 at Grantham and placed hurriedly on 55.019 at Darlington for the final run into York. A top speed of 98mph was reached despite running on one engine, and arrival at York at 23.06 was exactly on time.

The date of 2 January 1982 will always be remembered by 'Deltic' enthusiasts as the day on which their 'magic machines' bade farewell to British Rail. Here are a selection of pictures taken on the final day of operation.

Left:
The 'Deltic Scotsman Farewell' at Kings Cross shortly before departure. *R. Newling-Goode*

Above:
The 'Deltic Scotsman Farewell' passes through Selby, headed by 55.015 *Tulyar*. *G. S. Cutts*

Below:
55.015 *Tulyar* prepares to leave Finsbury Park depot for the last time. *C. W. Fellows*

55.019 was uncoupled and ran light to York depot to join 55.004, 55.007, 55.016 and 55.021. At midnight all the remaining 'Deltics' left in service apart from 55.002, 55.009, 55.015 and 55.022 were officially withdrawn from service.

The next day, 1 January 1982, the only 'Deltic' to move on the main line was 55.009, running light from Finsbury Park to Peterborough ready to act as standby locomotive for the final special the following day. It had been decided to send the crew from York to Peterborough on the stock that was forming the special (the stock coming from Heaton) rather than run 55.009 *Alycidon* to York. 55.015 *Tulyar* was prepared at Finsbury Park whose 'trademark' of white cab surrounds was applied, and 55.022 *Royal Scots Grey* waited at Haymarket for the final run from Edinburgh to Kings Cross.

The following day, Saturday 2 January 1982, was to see the end of the 'Deltic' era on British Rail. 55.015 left Kings Cross at 08.30 with the 'Deltic Scotsman Farewell', the final 'Deltic'-hauled train in British Rail service. It was booked for two stops at Doncaster and Newcastle for crew changes but was delayed at Newark after activating a hot axle detector at Balderton, which proved to be a false alarm: arrival at Edinburgh was a few minutes late because of this delay. 55.015 was removed from the train, its duties now finished, and ran light to Haymarket for fuel. 55.022 was then coupled to the train bearing a headboard which read 'Farewell To Thy Greatness', a sentiment echoed by every 'Deltic' enthusiast. The train left for the final run to Kings Cross at 14.30 and

55.015 followed light engine to York, including a stop-over at Gateshead on the way. Meanwhile 55.009, which had preceded the special on the outward leg from Peterborough to Newcastle, ran ahead of 55.022 as far as Peterborough and then returned to York, running on one engine as number two engine was low on coolant. 55.022 arrived at platform two at Kings Cross at 20.05 just three minutes late, witnessing emotional scenes. After release of the coaching stock, *Royal Scots Grey* pulled out of Kings Cross at 20.45 with horn blaring continuously and the enthusiasts lining the platforms cheering, clapping and crying. It disappeared into Gasworks Tunnel and the end of an era had passed.

55.022 ran light to Finsbury Park depot for fuel and then followed the 21.00 Kings Cross-Edinburgh train as far as Retford where it was able to pass through the centre road. It arrived at York depot shortly after midnight joining 55.004, 55.007, 55.009, 55.015, 55.016, 55.019 and 55.021. All 'Deltics' were now officially withdrawn from service. The three 'Deltics' still with nameplates on, 55.009, 55.015 and 55.022, had them removed on Sunday 3 January.

Above left:
55.022 prepares to leave Edinburgh Waverley on the return leg of the 'Deltic Scotsman Farewell'.
R. Newling-Goode

Left:
55.022 *Royal Scots Grey* at journey's end, Kings Cross. The emotion of 55.022's departure to Finsbury Park and York was overwhelming, and several people were reduced to tears by the occasion. *R. Newling-Goode*

Two views of the 'end of the Deltic era' at York depot at 01.30 on 3 January 1982.

Top:
55.019 and 55.015 head two rows of 'Deltics'.
C. W. Fellows

Above:
From left to right, 55.016, 55.009 (with 55.015 beyond), 55.019, 55.007 and 55.021. Four of these locomotives survived the cutter's torch. *C. W. Fellows*

2 After Withdrawal

On Monday 4 January 55.021, 55.007 and 55.019 were towed to Doncaster Works by 46.009, and the next day 55.004 was hauled away by 47.186, followed shortly by 47.552 hauling 55.016, 55.009, 55.015 and 55.022.

55.008, 55.013 and 55.017 remained at Finsbury Park for a few weeks because of a lack of locomotives or drivers to tow them away. They finally left on Saturday 22 January hauled by 40.020 on a 9G31 23.00 Finsbury Park-Doncaster freight special. For the record the formation was 40.020, 55.013, 55.008 and 55.017 plus brake van, and it left Finsbury Park at 22.55 travelling via Peterborough, Spalding, Sleaford and Lincoln to Doncaster Works. By now there were 16 'Deltics' in the plant although *Ballymoss* had almost been cut up.

During early January 55.015 was used as a power supply to test electric train heating on coaching stock as the static equipment was out of action, and on 21 January 55.019 was also used for this purpose.

During February tenders for sale were sent out for 'Deltics' Nos 4, 7, 8, 9, 10, 11, 13, 15, 16, 17, 19, 21 and 22 – 55.014 was in the process of being cut up. Due to an unprecedented demand by enthusiasts to visit Doncaster Works to see the 'Deltics', it was decided to hold a 'Deltic Farewell Open Day', which was arranged for Saturday 27 February. The 14 'Deltics' present in the scrap line were split up and arranged in the works yard, and 55.002 was towed from York to Doncaster by 20.064 on Friday 26 February to bring the number of 'Deltics' present to 15. Estimates vary as to the number of people who attended the open day, but it was somewhere around 14,000. Considering that the event was not publicised in the railway press, the number of people that did attend bears testament to the following these locomotives had. 55.002 returned light engine back to

York during the afternoon, defying the 'unofficial' preserved diesel ban on British Rail. For a short time it was positioned outside York depot, but was soon taken around to the National Railway Museum annexe.

55.010 and 55.021 were the next 'Deltics' to be cut up, but in early May the 'Deltic' Preservation Society purchased 55.009 for £16,550.09, and 55.019 for £16,550.19. The prices included air brake equipment (valued around £10,000 apiece), but scrap Class 37 bogies were placed under the locomotives. Both 'Deltics' needed attention in Doncaster Works before they left, but the Works was so busy that work wasn't carried out until July and August. They were finally handed over from British Rail to the 'Deltic' Preservation Society in a ceremony at Doncaster Works on Friday 20 August. Originally it was the intention for one 'Deltic' to tow the other to their new home on the North Yorkshire Moors Railway at Grosmont, but permission in the end was refused. Therefore 37.100 towed 55.009, 55.019 and brake van away from Doncaster Works on a '9X30' 14.00 Doncaster-Grosmont special freight. The 'Deltics' spent the night at Thornaby before carrying on to Grosmont, this time being towed by 37.005, and they finally arrived at Grosmont at 07.30 on the Saturday morning. The first 'Deltic' to run on the Moors railway was 55.019 with the 10.55 Grosmont-Pickering train and 12.20 return, followed later by 55.009 on the 14.55 Grosmont-Pickering train and 16.20 return.

Meanwhile other 'Deltics' continued to be cut up at Doncaster. Carlisle Upperby carriage depot arranged an open day for Saturday 11 September and the National Railway Museum was requested to send 55.002. For this reason *Kings Own Yorkshire Light Infantry* was towed to Dringhouses Yard on Thursday 9 September and placed dead inside 8N98, the 13.00 Healey Mills-Tyne. It went forward from there the

next morning dead inside 25.313 on 8M36, the 07.45 Tyne Yard-Carlisle. The 'Deltic' returned on Monday 13 September dead inside 37.071 on 8E14, the 11.35 Carlisle-Tyne Yard-Healey Mills as far as York.

One by one permission was granted for the

Below left:
55.017, 55.008 and 55.013 stand outside the works at Doncaster on 23 January 1982 after being towed from Finsbury Park overnight. *D. Cooper*

Above:
Some of the 14,000 crowd at the 'Deltic' open day on 27 February 1982. The locomotives are 55.011, 55.013, 55.008, 55.021 barely visible behind 55.017, 55.010 and 55.019. *R. Newling-Goode*

Below:
The scrap line at Doncaster on 7 February 1982: 55.005, 55.016, 55.009, 55.022, 55.004, 55.019, 55.010 and 55.021. *P. M. Marsh*

remaining 'Deltics' to be cut up. In December Christie's of London approached the Director of Supply at Derby with a view to auctioning a 'Deltic' locomotive together with various 'Deltic' parts, including nameplates. After inspection at Doncaster Works 55.015 *Tulyar* was chosen. A reserve price of £10,000 was placed on the locomotive but at the auction on 16 December the highest bid was only £5,500, so *Tulyar* was withdrawn from sale. On 21 January 1983 tenders were again sent out for 55.015 *Tulyar* and for 55.022 *Royal Scots Grey*, a new group to preserve 55.022 having already been established in the meantime.

55.002's next outing was an appearance at Workington Open Day on Saturday 10 September (20.001 hauled it from Dringhouses to Tyne Yard on Tuesday 6 September).

55.022 was officially handed over to 'Deltic' 9000 Limited at Doncaster Works on Wednesday 7 September 1983. The Nene Valley Railway at

Peterborough had offered a home for this 'Deltic' and so the next day 31.102 towed 55.022 (now renumbered 9000) to Peterborough via the joint line on a 7G30 09.30 Doncaster BREL-Peterborough West Yard freight special. At about 14.00 the Class 31 moved *Royal Scots Grey* from Peterborough diesel depot to Orton Mere where the 'Deltic' was detached to move under its own power to Wansford. On arrival at Wansford it was decided to run back to Orton Mere to check the opposite end's cab controls, before returning to Wansford where it arrived about 16.00. On Sunday 11 September 1983, 9000 worked two special test runs and carried shareholders, and members of the 'Deltic' 9000 Society and the Nene Valley Railway.

A fortnight later, on Saturday 24 September, Norwich Crown Point depot held an open day. No 9000, together with the steam locomotive *Britannia*, was towed from the Nene Valley Railway to Norwich by 31.415 on a '7G30' freight special on 22 September. The two returned to Peterborough on 26 September, hauled by 37.110 on a '9X81' special.

55.016 was secured for preservation by 'Deltic' 9000 Limited in early October. Purchased minus the air brake equipment it was seen as a valuable source of spares for 55.022, but was subsequently restored to full working order, and number two power-unit burst into life on Friday 15 March 1985 after being silent for over three years.

55.002's next celebrity appearance was at Ayr depot open days on Saturday 29 and Sunday 30 October.

Although permission had been granted for 55.015 *Tulyar* to be cut up there appeared to be some reluctance by the staff at Doncaster Works to do so. There were always rumours circulating about possible preservation and it wasn't until October 1983 that a private buyer was found for it. But before it entered preservation events took an unexpected turn in November when Derby Research Centre requested use of the locomotive for 'dynamic' and bogie tests. Freight advices were issued for it to be moved on Tuesday 15 November on a '9X19' freight special, but resources were not available. Another '9X19' advice for Thursday 17 November was issued, but again resources were not available. 55.015 finally moved from Doncaster Works behind 31.143 on Wednesday 23 November, leaving Doncaster at about 08.25.

Tulyar eventually moved to its new home at the Midland Railway Trust at Butterley on Saturday 4 February 1984, towed by 20.153 on a 9X30 08.45 Derby Research Centre-Ironville freight special. There 55.015 has been restored to full working order.

Doncaster Works arranged an open day for 28 July 1984 and No 9000 was to be one of the star attractions. For this reason the locomotive was towed from Peterborough to Doncaster on Thursday 26 July on a 9X31 11.00 Peterborough West Yard-Doncaster Works freight special hauled by 31.161, and returned to the Nene Valley Railway together with 55.016 on Monday 30 July hauled by 31.266 on a 9X32 10.20 Doncaster Works-Water Orton freight special.

No 9000's next celebrity appearance was at Perth Rail Fair on 13 April 1985. It was moved from the Nene Valley Railway on Tuesday 9 April and placed dead inside the train locomotive on 6S71, the 19.06 Whitemoor-Mossend (running as 6X71). No 9000 was detached at Millerhill on the Wednesday morning and towed to Haymarket depot for attention. Although it was planned for the locomotive to be conveyed on 6K25, the 03.45 Millerhill-Muir of Ord, as far as Perth, it was allowed to run light engine on Wednesday evening. At Perth British Rail used the 'Deltic' to shunt some stock from the sidings to the station, and to heat two Mk III sleepers, before moving to the exhibition site at Perth Yard. After the Rail Fair it towed a Class 27, a Class 20 and some stock from the yard to Perth station because of the failure of the Class

Above left:
The sad sight of 55.007 *Pinza* at the 'Deltic' open day.
P. Whitaker

Above:
55.002 passing through Selby on 27 February 1982 returning to York after appearing at the 'Deltic' open day at Doncaster Works. *C. W. Fellows*

Below:
All quiet at Doncaster the following day, with 55.011, 55.010, 55.016, 55.009, 55.019, 55.005 and 55.017. *C. W. Fellows*

27. No 9000 later returned to Haymarket, and then to Millerhill on Thursday 18 April, and was conveyed dead inside 37.024 on 6E89, the 14.26 Craiginches Yard-Immingham Reception Sidings (running as 6X89) as far as Doncaster. Here it was transferred to 6E86, the 19.20 Mossend-Parkeston (running as 6X86), hauled by 47.002, and detached at Peterborough Friday morning. No 9000 returned to the Nene Valley Railway later in the day.

Six out of 22 'Deltics' have been saved. It took over 2½ years for them all to reach their new homes and begin a new life. Let us hope they survive for many years to come.

Top left:
Three months after the open day, on 23 May, there were still nine 'Deltics' present in the scrap line: 55.004, 55.022, 55.016, 55.005, 55.013, 55.011, 55.017, 55.008 and 55.021. Work was shortly to commence on the cutting up of 55.007 *Pinza. C. W. Fellows*

Top:
55.009 and 55.019 are handed over to the 'Deltic' Preservation Society at Doncaster Works on 20 August 1982. *R. Newling-Goode*

Above left:
37.100 towing 55.009 and 55.019 past Dringhouses on 20 August 1982 en route from Doncaster Works to the North Yorkshire Moors Railway at Grosmont. *C. W. Fellows*

Above:
55.009 and 55.019 on their day of arrival at Grosmont. *C. W. Fellows*

Left:
The two 'Deltics' 'hide' in the tunnel at Grosmont in between duties on their first day of operation. *P. M. Marsh*

Above right:
The day after its arrival on the NYMR, 55.019 passes Ellerbeck with the 15.55 Grosmont-Pickering train. *W. A. Sharman*

Right:
55.009 rounds the curve at Beckhole on 26 August 1982 with the 13.55 Grosmont-Pickering train. *W. A. Sharman*

Left:
55.015 *Tulyar* outside the Derby Research Centre.
C. Oliphant

Below:
Scrap 'Deltic' engines at Doncaster Works on 26 April
1983. *G. W. Morrison*

Bottom:
45.043 hauls 55.002 'dead' in a freight train through
Hexham on 14 September 1983, returning to the NRM at
York after its appearance at Workington open day.
C. Oliphant

Right:
20.001 with 55.002 in tow departs Dringhouses, York for
Workington open day on 6 September 1983. *C. W. Fellows*

Below right:
No 9000 at Doncaster Works on 7 September 1983 being
handed over to 'Deltic' 9000 Limited. *G. W. Morrison*

Above left:
55.009 powers its way past Grosmont shed on 12 May 1984 with the 11.55 Grosmont-Pickering service. It has just connected with the 'Moors Explorer' special from London. *C. W. Fellows*

Left:
The great survivor, 55.016 *Gordon Highlander*, at Doncaster Works open day on 28 July 1984. *P. M. Marsh*

Above:
No 55.022 now once again carrying number 9000 starts up an engine at Perth Rail Fair on 13 April 1985. *C. Oliphant*

Right:
On 24 April 1985 the 'Deltic' Preservation Society carried out the first power-unit change on a 'Deltic' in preservation. Here the NYMR's 45-ton steam crane gently lowers replacement power-unit No 424 into 55.009 *Alycidon* at Pickering New Bridge yard. This is the site for a proposed 'Deltic' shed and museum to house 55.009 and 55.019, and hopefully one day the prototype 'Deltic'. *Yorkshire Evening Press*

Here we see 55.002 *King's Own Yorkshire Light Infantry* in beautiful condition at Workington on 10 September 1983. *A. J. Woof*

3 'Deltic' Workings from 4 October 1981

The following section dealing with all known 'Deltic' movements from Sunday 4 October, is based on our own and colleagues' records. It is inevitable that one or two errors may be included. Records for the first five weeks are not as detailed as the remaining period, as very detailed recordings were not started until November. All trains are shown by their headcodes (the train titles are listed overleaf), and if not working a train the status of 'Deltics' are also shown. Codes for stations and depots are also used (see list below).

Stations and Depots			
ABDN	Aberdeen	LS	Leeds
BDX	Bradford Exchange	MANCH	Manchester Victoria
BH	Barrow Hill	NCL	Newcastle
BOMO	Bournemouth	NL	Neville Hill
CARS	Carstairs	NRM	National Railway Museum
CSLE	Carlisle	PADD	Paddington
CY	Craigentinny	PD	Polmadie
DARL	Darlington	PE	Peterborough
DR	Doncaster	SCA	Scarborough
DR WKS	Doncaster Works	SF	Stratford
ED	Edinburgh	SKPT	Stockport
FP	Finsbury Park	WKW	Wakefield Westgate
GD	Gateshead	YK	York
GM	Grantham		
GLC	Glasgow Central	**Other abbreviations**	
HO	Holbeck	A/V	Available
HT	Heaton	E/F	Engine failure
KX	Kings Cross	EO	Electric only
LIV ST	Liverpool Street	OE	One engine
LPL	Liverpool	O/O/S	Out of service
		W	Withdrawn

TRAIN TITLES

1A01	07.00	Edinburgh-Aberdeen
1A08	08.07	York-Kings Cross
1A10 (SuO)	15.50	York-Kings Cross
1A19 (SuO)	19.13	York-Kings Cross
1A22	14.15	York-Kings Cross
1A26	15.50	York-Kings Cross
1A31	18.14	York-Kings Cross
1A34	20.19	York-Kings Cross
1A38	14.55	Edinburgh-Aberdeen
1A40	21.00	Newcastle-Kings Cross
1A40 (SuO)	21.28	Newcastle-Kings Cross
1A41	21.23	Bradford Exchange-Kings Cross
1A45	22.55	Newcastle-Kings Cross
1A55	14.05	Birmingham-Glasgow/Aberdeen
5A47	18.18	Clifton C/S-Ferme Park
1B13	07.00	Peterborough-Kings Cross
1B18	07.50	Peterborough-Kings Cross
1B21	17.17	Kings Cross-Peterborough
1B26	07.23	Peterborough-Kings Cross
1B50	02.00	Kings Cross-Peterborough
5B26	05.24	Kings Cross-Peterborough
1C83	08.08	Edinburgh-Carstairs
1C86	09.07	Edinburgh-Carstairs
1C91	10.25	Edinburgh-Carstairs
1C92	13.25	Edinburgh-Carstairs
1C94	17.35	Edinburgh-Carstairs
1C95	18.53	Edinburgh-Carstairs
1D08	19.40	Kings Cross-Hull
1E00	07.05	Liverpool-York
1E05	09.15	Edinburgh-Kings Cross
1E13	10.25	Aberdeen-Kings Cross
1E22 (SuO)	19.10	Liverpool-York
1E24	22.50	Shrewsbury-York
1E26	16.30	Aberdeen-York
1E29	17.18	Edinburgh-Newcastle
1E35 (SX)	20.25	Edinburgh-Kings Cross
1E35 (SO)	20.45	Edinburgh-Kings Cross
1E39 (SO)	22.15	Edinburgh-Kings Cross
1E39 (SX)	22.25	Edinburgh-Kings Cross

Above:
55.013 in wintry conditions passes Oakleigh Park on 13 December with the 10.05 Kings Cross-York train.
M. Lawrence

1E39 (SuO)	22.30	Edinburgh-Kings Cross		1M58	08.15	Newcastle-Liverpool
1E40 (SO)	19.15	Aberdeen-Kings Cross		1M62	08.50	York-Liverpool
1E40 (SX)	19.25	Aberdeen-Kings Cross		1M69 (SuO)	09.45	Edinburgh-Liverpool
1E42	23.15	Edinburgh-Kings Cross		1M70 (SuO)	15.40	York-Liverpool
1E43 (SO)	20.05	Aberdeen-Kings Cross		1M73	11.21	Newcastle-Liverpool
1E43 (SX)	20.35	Aberdeen-Kings Cross		1M76	15.50	York-Liverpool
1E48	21.20	Aberdeen-Kings Cross		1M77	15.18	Newcastle-Liverpool
1E50 (SuO)	21.15	Liverpool-York				
1E52	09.10	Dundee-Kings Cross		1N00	01.00	Kings Cross-Newcastle
1E59	18.05	Liverpool-York		1N03	21.20	Newcastle-Darlington
1E74	14.05	Liverpool-York		1N03 (SuO)	21.30	Newcastle-Darlington
1E89	20.40	Liverpool-York		1N04	07.15	Darlington-Newcastle
1E98	12.05	Liverpool-York		1N12	00.05	Kings Cross-Newcastle
1E99	13.05	Liverpool-York		1N14 (FO)	14.03	Kings Cross-Newcastle
5E27	21.34	Craigentinny-Ferme Park				
				1O54	18.00	Edinburgh-Glasgow Queen St
1G12	19.31	Carstairs-Edinburgh		1O61	19.30	Glasgow Queen St-Edinburgh
1G20 (SX)	18.23	Aberdeen-Edinburgh				
1G20 (SO)	18.30	Aberdeen-Edinburgh		1S08	07.05	Newcastle-Edinburgh
1G44	11.23	Carstairs-Edinburgh		1S12	05.50	Kings Cross-Aberdeen
1G83	17.15	Carstairs-Edinburgh		1S14	08.10	Newcastle-Edinburgh
2G18	07.25	Markinch-Edinburgh		1S15	15.53	Carlisle-Edinburgh
2G62	13.25	Dundee-Edinburgh		1S27	07.30	Plymouth-Edinburgh
5G18		Craigentinny-Markinch		1S27 (SuO)	11.25	Reading-Edinburgh
				1S37	07.37	Liverpool-Edinburgh
1L22	23.00	Kings Cross-Bradford Exchange		1S60	20.00	Kings Cross-Aberdeen
1L41	09.40	Kings Cross-York		1S66 (SX)	20.15	Kings Cross-Edinburgh
1L41 (SuO)	10.05	Kings Cross-York		1S66 (SO)	21.00	Kings Cross-Edinburgh
1L42 (SuO)	14.05	Kings Cross-York		1S70	22.15	Kings Cross-Aberdeen
1L43	14.03	Kings Cross-York		1S72	22.30	Kings Cross-Edinburgh
1L43 (SuO)	14.05	Kings Cross-York		1S72 (SuO)	22.40	Kings Cross-Edinburgh
1L44	16.03	Kings Cross-York		1S77	23.55	Kings Cross-Edinburgh
1L46 (SO)	23.00	Kings Cross-York		1S79	23.20	Kings Cross-Aberdeen
2L36	11.25	Edinburgh-Dundee				
5L01	15.54	Neville Hill-York		1V93	09.50	Edinburgh-Plymouth
5L04	23.30	Hull-York		1V93 (SuO)	12.25	Newcastle-Plymouth
				5V44	12.35	Edinburgh-Polmadie
1M04	07.18	Edinburgh-Carlisle				
1M26	13.50	York-Liverpool		5Z20	07.35	Edinburgh-Aberdeen
1M41	22.08	York-Shrewsbury				(Mk 3 sleepers)
1M53	07.49	York-Liverpool				

	55.002	55.004	55.007	55.008	55.009	55.010	55.011
SUNDAY 4 OCTOBER	YK	YK	1V93 TO YK	YK	FP 'OE'	1L43	1A40 'OE'
MONDAY 5 OCTOBER	YK	YK	1M62 1E99 5A47 1S79 TO ED	1A22 1D08 5L04	1N12 1S14 1E29 1A45 'OE'	1A08 1L44	5B26 1B26 'OE'
TUESDAY 6 OCTOBER	YK	YK	1V93 TO YK	1A22 1S70 TO ED	1D08 5L04	1A08 1L44 1A34	1N12 0L01 TO YK 0B02 TO FP 'OE'
WEDNESDAY 7 OCTOBER	YK	YK	1A08 1L44 1A34	1V93 TO YK 1S27	YK	1S12 TO NCL 0L01 TO YK 1A26	1N00 1S08 1E29 'OE'
THURSDAY 8 OCTOBER	YK	YK	1L41 1A22 1S60 TO ED	1E48 1S70 TO NCL E/F	1A08 1D08 5L04	1N12 TO DR 0B02 TO FP 1L43 1A31	1E42 1L22 'OE'
FRIDAY 9 OCTOBER	YK	YK	1M04 1S15	GD 0L01 TO YK 'OE'	YK	1N12 1S12 TO ED 1E29 1A45	0L50 TO HO 0L01 TO YK 1A26 1L22 'OE'
SATURDAY 10 OCTOBER	1Z73 YK-ED 1Z73 ED-YK	YK	0C01 1Z70 1E29	YK 'OE'	YK	1L46	0L50 TO HO 0L01 TO YK 'OE'
SUNDAY 11 OCTOBER	YK	YK	GD 1A40	YK 'OE'	YK	YK	YK 'OE'
MONDAY 12 OCTOBER	YK	YK	5B26 1B26	YK 'OE'	YK	1A26 1S79 TO ED	YK 'OE'
TUESDAY 13 OCTOBER	YK	YK	1N00 TO YK 1A40	YK 'OE'	YK	1V93 TO YK 1S27 1E35	1M62 1E99 0B02 TO FP 1S79 TO ED 'OE'
WEDNESDAY 14 OCTOBER	YK	1A40	1L41 1A22 1D08 5L04	1M62 1E99 0B02 TO FP 'OE'	YK	1L43 1A31	1V93 TO YK 1S27 1E39 'OE'
THURSDAY 15 OCTOBER	YK	5B26 1B26 1L43 1A31	1A08	FP 1D08 5L04 'OE'	YK	1S12 TO ED 1E35	FP 'OE'
FRIDAY 16 OCTOBER	1M62 1E74	1L41 1A22 1S70 TO ED	1N12 'OE'	0L01 TO NL 5A31 TO YK 1N14 1A45 'OE'	1S60 TO NCL	1N14 TO YK 1A31 1S77	1S72 TO YK 'OE'
SATURDAY 17 OCTOBER	0L01 TO YK	1V93 TO YK 1S27 1E43	1S14 1E29 1E43	FP 'OE'	1F52 TO PERTH 0F52 TO ABDN 1F52 TO NCL	HA	YK 'OE'

55.013	55.014	55.015	55.016	55.017	55.018	55.019	55.021	55.022
5A47	1S72 1E42	1E43 TO NCL	YK	1E40	YK	BH (Open Day) 'OE'	1L22 0L01 TO YK 'OE'	SF
1L22 0L01 TO YK	1L41 YK	1A40	1A34	1L43 1A31	YK 'EO'	BH 0L01 TO YK 'OE'	0D01 TO DR 'OE'	SF
YK	1A26 1S77	5B26 1B26 FP	1S12 TO NCL 0L01 TO YK 1S27	1N00 1S08 1E40	YK 'EO'	0D01 TO DR WKS 'OE'	DR WKS	SF
0B02 TO FP 1L43 1A31	1A38 1G20 1E43	FP	IE 1S79	FP	0B06 TO PE 0B02 TO FP 1S70 TO ED 'EO'	DR WKS	DR WKS	SF
1B50 1B13 1S77	1L44 1A34	FP	1C86 1G44 1A38 1G20 1E42	1N00 1S08 1C94 1G12 1E35	1V93 TO YK 1S27 'EO'	DR WKS	DR WKS	SF
1V93 TO YK 1S27 1E39 TO NCL	1N00 1S08 1E35	FP	1S70 TO ED	1N14 TO YK 1A31	1E48 1L44 1A34 'EO'	DR WKS	DR WKS	SF
1S14 1A38 1G20 1E40	1L43 1A31	FP	1V93 TO YK 1S27 1E39	1N12 0L01 TO YK	1S12 TO ED 'EO'	DR WKS	DR WKS	SF
1S60 TO ED	1L41 1A10 1S70 TO ED	FP	1L42 1A19	YK	1V93 TO YK 1S27 'EO'	DR WKS	DR WKS	SF
1G18 2G18 1E35	1V93 TO YK 1S27 1E40	FP	FP	1A08 1L44 1A34	1E48 1D08 TO DR 0L01 TO YK 'EO' 'OE'	DR WKS	DR WKS	SF
1D08 1L04	1S66 TO YK	1L44 1A34	FP	1S12 TO ED 1E29 1A45	YK 'EO' 'OE'	DR WKS	DR WKS	0L01 TO FP
YK	1A26 1S70 TO ED	FP	FP	5B26 1B26 1S66	YK 'EO' 'OE'	DR WKS	DR WKS	FP
1A26 1S70 TO ED	1V93 1S27 1E42	FP	FP	HA	YK 'EO' 'OE'	DR WKS	DR WKS	FP
1V93 TO YK 1S27 1E42	FP	FP	FP	1E29 1N03 0L01 TO YK	YK 'EO' 'OE'	DR WKS	0B06 TO PE 0B02 TO FP 1D08 5L04	FP
1L43 1A31	1N12 0L01 TO YK	1Z47 FP-BOMO 1Z47 BOMO-FP	FP	YK	YK 'EO' 'OE'	DR WKS	1Z42 YK-SCA 1Z42 SCA-YK	FP

	55.002	55.004	55.007	55.008	55.009	55.010	55.011
SUNDAY 18 OCTOBER	YK	FP 1S70 TO ED	1A40 'OE'	1N12 TO PE 'OE'	1M73 TO YK	1E40	YK 'OE'
MONDAY 19 OCTOBER	YK	1V93 TO YK 1S27 1E35	5B26 1B26 'OE'	0B02 TO FP 1D08 5L04 'OE'	YK	1N00 1S08 1E29 1A45	0B02 TO FP 1S72 'OE'
TUESDAY 20 OCTOBER	1M62 1E99	1D08 5L04	1N12 0L01 TO YK 'OE'	1M26 1E59 'OE'	YK	1L44 1A34	1E29 1A45 'OE'
WEDNESDAY 21 OCTOBER	YK	YK	YK 'OE'	1M62 1E99 'OE'	YK	1L41 1A22 1S79	FP 'OE'
THURSDAY 22 OCTOBER	YK	1A22 1D08 5L04	YK 'OE'	YK 'OE'	1A08 1L44	1V93 TO YK 1S27 1E39	FP 'OE'
FRIDAY 23 OCTOBER	YK	1A08 1N14 TO YK 1A31 1S77	TOWED TO SF 'OE'	YK 'OE'	YK	FP	1N12 1S14 1E29 1A45 'OE'
SATURDAY 24 OCTOBER	YK	1V93 TO YK 1S27 1E39	SF	YK 'OE'	YK	FP	FP 'OE'

Below:
55.015 passing Southampton on its way to Bournemouth with the 'Wessex Deltic' on 17 October 1981.   *J. Sparks*

55.013	55.014	55.015	55.016	55.017	55.018	55.019	55.021	55.022
1L41 1A10	YK	1L42	FP	1A19	YK	DR WKS	0B02 TO FP 1S79 TO ED	FP
1L41 1A22 1S70	1A08 1L44 1A34	YK	FP 'OE'	1L43 1A31 1S77	YK W	DR WKS	1E39	FP
1M04 1S15	1S12 TO NCL 0L01 TO YK 1A26 1S77	YK	1N00 1S08 1E35 TO NCL 'OE'	1V93 TO YK 1S27 1E39	YK TOWED TO SF W	DR WKS	1S70 TO ED	FP
1E43 1L44 1A34	1V93 TO YK 1S27 1E35	YK	1S14 1E29 1A45 'OE'	1L43 YK	SF W	DR WKS	1M04 1S15 1E39	1D08 TO PE (E/F) 0B02 TO FP
1S12 TO NCL 0L01 TO YK 1A26	FP	1M62 1E99 1M76 1E89	5B26 1B26 'OE'	YK 1A34	SF W	DR WKS	1S70 TO ED	FP 1L43 1A31
1S12 TO NCL 0L01 TO YK 1A26 1S70 TO ED	FP	YK 0L01 TO NL	1N00 1S08 'OE'	FP	SF W	DR WKS	1V93 TO YK 1S27 1E35	FP 1L44 1A34
HA E35	FP	5F50 TO YK 1F50 TO ABDN 1F50 TO YK 5F50 TO NL	1E29 'OE'	1L43 1A31	SF W	DR WKS	1Z30 TO LS* 0D01 TO DR 9Z11 21-35 Crofton- Gascoigne-Wood	1S12 TO NCL 0L01 TO YK
								*(08.45 KX-BLACKPOOL EXC)

Below:
55.022 and 55.009 stand outside York depot on 3 November. *P. Gash*

	55.002	55.004	55.007	55.008	55.009	55.010	55.011
SUNDAY 25 OCTOBER	YK	FP	SF	YK 'OE'	YK	FP	1N12 1N03 0L01 TO YK 'OE'
MONDAY 26 OCTOBER	YK	1N00 1S08 1E35	SF	YK 'OE'	YK	1L43 1A31	1M62 1E99 'OE'
TUESDAY 27 OCTOBER	YK	1L41 1A22 1D08 5L04	SF	YK 'OE'	YK	1N00 1S08 1E35	1M62 1E99 1M76 1E89 'OE'
WEDNESDAY 28 OCTOBER	YK	1M53 1E98 1M76 LPL(E/F) 'OE'	SF	YK 'OE'	YK	1L41 1A22 1D08 5L04	1M62 1E99 1M77 1E89 'OE'
THURSDAY 29 OCTOBER	1M62 1E99	TOWED TO YK YK 'OE'	SF	0B02 TO PE 0S79 TO FP 'OE'	YK	YK	YK 'OE'
FRIDAY 30 OCTOBER	YK 0B02 TO FP	TOWED TO SF 'OE'	0B02 TO FP	1N00 TO YK 'OE'	YK	1A08 1L44 1A34	YK 1N14 1A45 'OE'
SATURDAY 31 OCTOBER	1F52 TO ED 1F52 TO PE 5F52 TO KX	SF 'OE'	FP	1A31 'OE'	YK	1S12 TO NCL 0L01 TO YK 1A26	FP 'OE'
SUNDAY 1 NOVEMBER	1L42	SF	FP	FP 0L01 TO SF 'OE'	YK	FP	1N12 1N03 0L01 TO YK 'OE'
MONDAY 2 NOVEMBER	YK	SF W	1L43 1A31 1S77	SF 'OE'	YK	1L41 1A22 1D08 5L04	YK 'OE'
TUESDAY 3 NOVEMBER	YK	SF W	1E35	SF 'OE'	YK	0B02 TO FP 1S72	YK 'OE'
WEDNESDAY 4 NOVEMBER	YK	SF W	1L41 1A22 1D08 5L04	SF 'OE'	YK	HA 1E35	YK 0B02 TO FP 1S72 'OE'
THURSDAY 5 NOVEMBER	YK	SF W	1A08 1L44 1A34	SF 'OE'	YK	1L43 1A31 1S77	1E29 1A45 'OE'
FRIDAY 6 NOVEMBER	1A26 1S70 TO ED	SF W	1S12 1E26	SF 'OE'	YK	HA 1E35	0C01 TO SF 'OE'
SATURDAY 7 NOVEMBER	1F51 TO KX	SF W	1A08 1L43 1A31	SF 'OE'	YK	FP 1S72	SF 'OE'

55.013	55.014	55.015	55.016	55.017	55.018	55.019	55.021	55.022
FP	FP	0L01 TO YK	1A40 'OE'	1L41 1A10 1S72	SF W	DR WKS	0B02 TO FP 1S77	YK
1N12 1S14 1E39	FP	YK	5B26 1B26 1S77 'OE'	1V93 TO YK 1S27 1E43	SF W	DR WKS	1E29 1A45	YK
FP	FP	YK	HA 1E39 'OE'	1L44 1A34	SF W	DR WKS	1L43 1M41 TO SKPT	YK
1N00 1S08 1E35	FP	YK	FP 'OE'	1S12 TO NCL 0L01 TO YK 0B02 TO FP 1L22	SF W	DR WKS	1E24 1A26	YK
FP 1S66	FP	YK	1N00 1S08 1C92 1G83 1E39 'OE'	0L50 TO HO 0L01 TO YK 1A22 1D08 5L04	SF W	DR WKS	1N12 0L01 1A26 1S70	YK
1M04 1S15 1E43	1N14 TO YK 1A31 1S77 TO YK	YK	1S72 'OE'	YK 'OE'	SF W	DR WKS	1V93 TO YK 1S27 1E42	YK
FP 1S72	1A08 1L44	YK	1E26 'OE'	YK 'OE'	SF W	DR WKS	FP	YK
HA 1E40	1A19	YK	YK 'OE'	YK 'OE'	SF W	DR WKS	FP 1S70	YK
FP	1S12 TO ED	YK	YK 'OE'	YK 'OE'	SF W	DR WKS	1M04 1S15 1E39 TO NCL	YK
FP	1E48 1L44 1A34	YK	1A08 1L43 1A31	1N12 1A40 'OE'	SF W	DR WKS	GD 1A45	YK
1L43 1A31	1S12 1E26	1A08 1L44	1N12 1N03 0L01 TO YK	5B26 1B26 1S66 'OE'	SF W	DR WKS	FP	1M62 1E99 (E/F at MANCH)
1S12 TO NCL 0L01 TO YK 1A26 1S79 TO ED	YK	YK	YK	1M04 1S15 1E39 'OE'	SF W	DR WKS	1N00 1S08 1E35	YK 'OE'
HA 1E29 1A45	1S60 TO NCL	0B02 TO FP	YK	FP 'OE'	SF W	DR WKS	1N14 TO YK 1A31 1S77	0B02 TO FP 0L01 TO SF 'OE'
1L44	GD	1F51 TO ED 1E39	YK	1N12 GD 'OE'	SF W	DR WKS	1E29	SF 'OE'

	55.002	55.004	55.007	55.008	55.009	55.010	55.011
SUNDAY 8 NOVEMBER	1L41 1A10 1S70 TO ED	SF W	O/O/S FP 1S79 TO ED	O/O/S SF 'OE'	O/O/S YK	HA 1E35	SF 'OE'
MONDAY 9 NOVEMBER	1M04 1S15 1E39	SF W	HA 1E35	O/O/S SF 'OE'	O/O/S YK	1L43 1A31	SF W
TUESDAY 10 NOVEMBER	1L43 1A31	SF W	1L41 1A22 1D08 5L04	O/O/S SF 'OE'	O/O/S YK	1N00 1S08 1E29 1A45	SF W
WEDNESDAY 11 NOVEMBER	O/O/S FP	SF W	1A08 1L44 1A34	O/O/S SF 'OE'	O/O/S YK	1L41 1A26 1S70 TO ED	SF W
THURSDAY 12 NOVEMBER	TOWED FP-YK BY 55015	SF W	1S12 TO YK 0B06 TO PE 0B02 TO FP 1S72	0L01 TO FP 1L44	1M62 1E99	1M04 1S15 1E39	SF W
FRIDAY 13 NOVEMBER	O/O/S YK	SF W	HA 1E35	1A08 1L44 1A34	1A26	1N14 TO YK 1A31 1S77	SF W
SATURDAY 14 NOVEMBER	O/O/S YK	SF W	1L43 1A31	A/V FP	1Z37 TO CSLE 1Z37 TO KX	A/V HA 'OE'	SF W
SUNDAY 15 NOVEMBER	O/O/S YK	SF W	1L42 1A19 'EO'	1N12 GD	A/V FP	1E48 TO DREM E/F 0E48 TO HA O/O/S HA	SF W
MONDAY 16 NOVEMBER	O/O/S YK	SF W	5B26 1B26 1S70 TO ED 'EO'	1E48 1L44 1A34 'EO'	1N12 1S14 1E35	O/O/S HA	SF W
TUESDAY 17 NOVEMBER	O/O/S YK	SF W	5G18 2G18 1A38 1G20 'EO'	1S12 TO NCL 0L01 TO YK 1A22 1D08 5L04	1L41 1A26 1S70 TO ED	TOWED TO YK BY 40 033 O/O/S YK	SF W
WEDNESDAY 18 NOVEMBER	1M62 1E99 O/O/S YK	SF W	1E48 O/O/S FP 'EO'	1A26 1S77	1F50 07.00 ED-KX (CHARTER) 1S60 TO YK E/F	O/O/S YK	SF W
THURSDAY 19 NOVEMBER	1M76 1E59	SF W	O/O/S FP 'EO'	HA 1E35	O/O/S YK	O/O/S YK	SF W
FRIDAY 20 NOVEMBER	O/O/S YK	SF W	O/O/S FP	1L41 1A22 1D08 5L04	O/O/S YK	O/O/S YK	SF W
SATURDAY 21 NOVEMBER	1Z10 TO ED 1E40	SF W	O/O/S FP	O/O/S YK	O/O/S YK	1A08 1L43 1A31	SF W

55.013	55.014	55.015	55.016	55.017	55.018	55.019	55.021	55.022
O/O/S YK	O/O/S GD	O/O/S FP	O/O/S YK	A/V GD 'OE'	SF W	O/O/S DR WKS	0L01 TO YK 1A19	O/O/S SF 'OE'
1A22 1D08 5L04	O/O/S GD	O/O/S FP	1A26 1S70 TO ED	1A40 TO YK 'OE'	SF W	O/O/S DR WKS	1N00 1S08 1E29 1A45 'OE'	O/O/S SF 'OE'
1A08 1S77	1S14 (E/F AT CRAMLINGTON) O/O/S HA	O/O/S FP	1C86 1G44 1A38 1G20	1A26 1S70 TO PE 'OE'	SF W	0L01 TO Ponton ASSISTED 6C30 TO PE 1S70 TO NCL	1L44 1A34	O/O/S SF 'OE'
HA 1E35 TO YK	TOWED TO YK O/O/S YK	O/O/S FP	1E48 1L43 1A31	1A40 5B26 1B26 'OE'	SF W	1M04 1S15 TO NCL	1S12 TO NCL 0L01 TO YK 1A22 1S77	O/O/S SF 'OE'
1A26	O/O/S YK	0L01 TO YK (TOWING 55 002)	5B26 1B26 1L43 1A31	1N12 0L01 TO DR 'OE'	SF W	0L01 TO YK O/O/S YK	1S12 1E26	0L01 TO FP 1S70 TO NCL
1N12 1S14 1E39	O/O/S YK	O/O/S YK	1L41 1A22 1D08 5L04	O/O/S DR WKS	SF W	0B06 TO-PE 0B02 TO-FP	O/O/S YK	0L01 TO YK O/O/S YK
FP 1S60 TO ED	O/O/S YK	O/O/S YK	1A08 1L44	O/O/S DR WKS	SF W	1S12 TO YK (ASSISTED BY 31175 FROM PE) O/O/S YK	1A26	O/O/S YK
HA 1E39	O/O/S YK	O/O/S YK	1E35	DR WKS	SF W	O/O/S YK	1L41 YK	O/O/S YK
FP 1S66	O/O/S YK	O/O/S YK	1N00 1S08 1E29 1A45	DR WKS	SF W	O/O/S YK	1A08 1L43 1A31 1S77	O/O/S YK
1M04 1S15 1E40	O/O/S YK	O/O/S YK	1L43 1A31 1S77	DR WKS	SF W	1A08 1L44 1A34	HA 1E35	O/O/S YK
1L44 1A34	O/O/S YK	1A08 O/O/S FP	HA 1E35	0802 TO FP 1S60 TO YK E/F	SF W	1L41 1A22 1D08 5L04	1L43 1A31	O/O/S YK
1S12 TO ED 1E39	O/O/S YK	FP 1S66	1L41 1A22 1D08 5L04	O/O/S YK	SF W	1E42 1L43 1A31 1S77	1N00 1S08 1E29 1A45	O/O/S YK
1L43 1A31	O/O/S YK	1M04 1S15 1E39	O/O/S YK	O/O/S YK	SF W	HA 1E35	1L44 1E34	1M62 TO LS E/F 0L01 TO YK
1N12 1S14 1Z10 TO YK	O/O/S YK	O/O/S FP	0L01 TO NL 5G08 TO YK 1G08 07-43 YK-KX (CHARTER) 1L44	0B02 TO FP 1G08 19-35 KX-YKW (CHARTER) 5G08 TO NL 0L01 TO YK	SF	O/O/S FP	1N00 1S08 1F1112.15ED-NCL 5F11 TO CY 1E35	O/O/S YK

	55.002	55.004	55.007	55.008	55.009	55.010	55.011
SUNDAY 22 NOVEMBER	O/O/S FP 1S72 'OE'	SF W	O/O/S FP	1A19	O/O/S YK	A/V FP 1S77 TO ED	SF W
MONDAY 23 NOVEMBER	1E29 1N03 'OE'	TOWED TO YK IN 9G36 W	O/O/S FP	1NDO 1S08 1E35	O/O/S YK	1C86 1S37 1A38 1G20	TOWED TO YK IN 9G36 W
TUESDAY 24 NOVEMBER	0L01 TO YK TOWED 55014 AND 40058 TO SF 'OE'	YK W	O/O/S FP	1S12 TO DR* 0B02 TO FP 1L43 1A31 1S77	O/O/S YK	1E48 1B21 0B01 TO FP 1S72	TOWED TO DR IN 9G36 TOWED TO DR WKS W
WEDNESDAY 25 NOVEMBER	O/O/S SF	YK W	1L41 1A22 1D08 5L04	1E29 1A45	1M62 1E99	1C83 1G44 1A38 1G20	DR WKS W
THURSDAY 26 NOVEMBER	O/O/S SF 0L01 TO FP O/O/S FP	YK W	1A26 1S77	5B26 1B26 1S66	O/O/S YK	1E43 1S60 TO ED	DR WKS W
FRIDAY 27 NOVEMBER	1L41 1A22	YK W	A/V HA 1E40	1M04 1S15 1E42	0L01 TO NL 5L01 TO YK 0L01 TO GD	5G18 2G18/1C91 1S37 1A38 1G20	DR WKS W
SATURDAY 28 NOVEMBER	O/O/S FP	YK W	A/V FP 1S60 TO ED	1L44 O/O/S YK	1Z11 TO ED 1Z11 TO NCL 1A40	1E43 1L46 TO DR	DR WKS W
SUNDAY 29 NOVEMBER	O/O/S FP 'OE'	YK W	A/V HA 1E40	O/O/S YK	1L41 YK	1E40 FP	
MONDAY 30 NOVEMBER	O/O/S FP 'OE'	YK W	O/O/S FP 1S60 TO ED	O/O/S YK	O/O/S YK	1N12 0L01 TO YK 1A31 1S77	
TUESDAY 1 DECEMBER	O/O/S FP 0L01 TO SF O/O/S SF 'OE'	YK W	5G18 2G18 1S12 1E26	O/O/S YK 'EO'	O/O/S YK	0L01 TO GD 0L01 TO YK 1A26	
WEDNESDAY 2 DECEMBER	O/O/S SF 'OE'	YK W	1A26 1S70 TO ED	1A08 1L44 1A34 'EO'	O/O/S YK	O/O/S FP	
THURSDAY 3 DECEMBER	O/O/S SF 'OE'	YK W	1M04 1S15	1S12 1E26 'EO'	1M62 1E99 O/O/S YK	1N00 1S08 O/O/S HA 1E35	
FRIDAY 4 DECEMBER	0L01 TO FP O/O/S FP	YK W	1E43 1N14 TO YK 1A31	1A08 1L44 0D01 TO DR 1S66 'EO'	O/O/S YK	1L41 1A22 1D08 5L04	
SATURDAY 5 DECEMBER	O/O/S FP	YK W	1S12 TO NCL 0L01 TO YK 1M76 1E89	A/V HA 'EO'	O/O/S YK	O/O/S YK 1A26	

*(46.046 ASSISTING FROM PE, LOW FUEL)

55.013	55.014	55.015	55.016	55.017	55.018	55.019	55.021	55.022
O/O/S YK	O/O/S YK	O/O/S FP	A/V YK	A/V YK 0B02 TO PE	SF W	A/V FP 1S70 TO ED	O/O/S FP 1S77 TO ED	O/O/S YK
O/O/S YK	YK W	O/O/S FP	1A08 1L44 1A34	1B18 1B21 0B02 TO FP 1S72	TOWED TO YK IN 9G36 W	1M04 1S15	1F55 ED-GLC (JOBS EXPRESS CHARTER) 0F55 TO HA 1E39	1M62 1E99
1A08 1L44 1A34	TOWED TO SF BY 55 002 W	O/O/S FP	O/O/S FP	A/V HA 1E35	TOWED TO DR IN 9G36 Towed to DR WKS W	1E43 FP 1S60 TO ED	1L41 1A22 1D08 5L04	O/O/S YK
1S12 1E26	SF W	O/O/S FP	O/O/S FP	1L43 1A31 'EO'	DR WKS W	HA 1E35	0L01 TO THIRSK 0L01 TO YK (TRIAL) 1A26 1S79	O/O/S YK
1A08 O/O/S FP 1S79 TO ED	SF W	O/O/S FP	1L44 1A34	1S12 TO NCL 0L01 TO YK 1A22 1D08/5L04 'EO'	DR WKS W	1L43 1A31	A/V HA 1E29 1A45	1M62 1E99 O/O/S YK
A/V HA 1E29 1A45	SF W	O/O/S FP	1S12 TO ED 1E35	1A08 1L44 1A34 'EO'	DR WKS W	1N14	A/V FP 1D08 5L04	O/O/S YK
A/V FP 1S66	SF W	O/O/S FP	1Z40 TO EXETER 1Z40 TO LIV. ST 0C01 TO SF	1S12 TO ED O/O/S HA 'EO'	DR WKS W	1S60 TO ED 1M04 1S15	O/O/S YK	1Z38 TO PADD 1Z38 TO YK
A/V HA 1E39	SF W	O/O/S FP	A/V SF	O/O/S HA 'EO'		1E43 1L42 1A19	O/O/S YK 1A10 E/F KX (FIRE) TOWED TO FP	O/O/S YK
O/O/S FP 1S66	SF W	O/O/S FP 1L43 A/V YK	0B01 TO FP 1S72	1E48 1L44 1A34 'EO'		1N00 1S08 0C00 TO CARS To tow '47' to HA 1E35	O/O/S FP	O/O/S YK
1M04 1S15 1E40	SF W	1A08 1D08 5L04	1C86 1G44 1A38 1G20	1L41 1A22 1S70 TO ED 'EO'		O/O/S FP	O/O/S FP	O/O/S YK
O/O/S FP 1S77 ('OE' EX DR)	SF W	1M62 1E99 1M76 1E89	1M04 1S15 1E39	5V44 TO PD 5G00 TO ED 'EO'		O/O/S FP	A/V FP 'OE'	O/O/S YK
1C91 1G44 1E29 'OE'	SF W	O/O/S YK	1L43 1A31 1S77	1E48 1L44 O/O/S YK 'EO'		O/O/S FP	1N12 0L01 TO YK 'OE'	O/O/S YK
1S60 TO ED 1E29 1A45 'OE'	SF W	O/O/S YK 0B01 TO FP	A/V HA 1E35	O/O/S YK 'EO'		O/O/S FP	A/V YK 1A34	1M62 1E99 O/O/S YK
A/V FP 'OE'	TOWED TO DR WKS BY 37 004 W	1B50 1Z35 TO CSLE 1Z35 TO PE	A/V FP	1A08 1L44 'EO'		1N12 1S12 TO ED 1E35	1L43 O/O/S YK	O/O/S YK

	55.002	55.004	55.007	55.008	55.009	55.010	55.011
SUNDAY 6 DECEMBER	O/O/S FP 1S70 TO ED	YK W	O/O/S YK	A/V HA 'EO'	O/O/S YK	O/O/S FP 1S60 TO ED	
MONDAY 7 DECEMBER	A/V HA 1E35	YK W	O/O/S YK	1E48 1L43 1A31 'EO'	O/O/S YK	1M04 1S15 'OE'	
TUESDAY 8 DECEMBER	1L41 1A22	YK W	O/O/S YK	1S12 TO ED 1A38 1G20 'EO'	O/O/S YK	1E43 TO DR E/F O/O/S DR 0L01 TO YK	
WEDNESDAY 9 DECEMBER	1N12 1M04 1S15 1E39	YK W	O/O/S YK 1A26 1S70 TO YK (47 416 ASSISTED FROM GM)	1E48 O/O/S FP 'EO'	O/O/S YK	O/O/S YK 0B06 TO PE 0S79 to HITCHIN 1S60 TO ED (Asst 47 417 to PE)	
THURSDAY 10 DECEMBER	O/O/S FP	YK W	O/O/S YK 1A08 1S66 TO NCL	1S12 TO ED O/O/S HA 'EO'	1M62 1E99 0B06 TO PE 0B02 TO FP 1S77 TO ED	A/V HA 1E29 (E/F AT HT 40068 ASSIST TO NCL) O/O/S GD	
FRIDAY 11 DECEMBER	O/O/S FP	YK W	E/F NCL O/O/S GD	1E48 A/V FP 1S70 TO ED 'EO'	2L36 2G62 1A38 1G20	1S08 1E29 1A45 TO DR E/F O/O/S DR	
SATURDAY 12 DECEMBER	1B50 0G06 TO NRW 1G06 TO YK 1G06 TO NRW	YK W	5F05 TO ED 1E05 TO NCL 1M77 1E89	1A01 1E13 TO ED 'EO'	1Z55 TO ABDN 1Z55 TO ED 1E35	0L01 TO YK O/O/S YK A/V YK 'OE'	
SUNDAY 13 DECEMBER	A/V NRW	YK W	O/O/S YK	A/V HA 'EO'	O/O/S FP 1S70 TO ED	A/V YK 1M70 1E50 'OE'	
MONDAY 14 DECEMBER	A/V NRW	YK W	O/O/S YK 1S79 TO ED 1E29 O/O/S GD	A/V HA 1E26 'EO'	1E13 TO YK 0E74 to TOLLER- TON 1E74 (ASSISTING 47- 444) A/V GD	1M62 1E99 O/O/S YK 'OE'	
TUESDAY 15 DECEMBER	0B01 TO PE 0B02 TO FP 1S77 TO NCL	YK W	O/O/S GD 1M58 TO LS 0L01 TO YK 1A26 1S79 TO NCL	1A08 1L44 1A34 'EO'	1S60 TO ED 1M04 1S15 1E39	O/O/S YK 'OE'	
WEDNESDAY 16 DECEMBER	1S14 O/O/S HA 1A38 1G20	YK W	E/F NCL O/O/S GD	1S12 1E26 'EO'	O/O/S FP 1L44 1A34	O/O/S YK 'OE'	
THURSDAY 17 DECEMBER	1E43 TO YK E/F O/O/S YK	YK W	O/O/S GD A/V GD 'OE'	1A08 TO PE E/F 5G08 TO KX 1S70 TO ED 'EO'	1S12 TO ED A/V HA 1E35 TO DR	O/O/S YK 1M41 TO SKPT 'OE'	
FRIDAY 18 DECEMBER	O/O/S YK	YK W	0N04 TO DARL 1N04 1N03 'OE'	A/V HA 'EO'	E/F DR O/O/S DR 0B01 TO FP O/O/S FP	1E24 TO LS A/V HO 1E00 1A26 1S79 TO NCL 'OE'	
SATURDAY 19 DECEMBER	1Z25 TO SCA 1Z25 TO DR 0L01 TO YK	YK W	0L01 TO YK O/O/S YK 'OE'	O/O/S HA 1A38 1G20 'EO'	1G10 TO NRW 1G10 TO LIV.ST 0C00 TO SF	1M73 TO YK A/V YK 'OE'	

* (E/F AT AYCLIFFE, 45.076 ASSISTED TO NCL)

55.013	55.014	55.015	55.016	55.017	55.018	55.019	55.021	55.022
1N12 1A40 TO YK E/F O/O/S YK		O/O/S PE 0B01 TO KX 1S77	1L41 1A10 O/O/S FP	A/V YK 1A19 'EO'		O/O/S FP 1S72	O/O/S YK	O/O/S YK
O/O/S YK		A/V HA 1E29 1A45	O/O/S FP	1S12 TO NCL 0L01 TO YK 1A22 1D08 5L04/'EO'		A/V HA 1E40	1A08 1L44 1A34	O/O/S YK
O/O/S YK		1L43 1A31 1S77	O/O/S FP 1B21 0B00 TO KX 1S72	1A08 1L44 1A34 'EO'		A/V FP 1S66	0B00 TO PE 1B18 1S60 TO YK E/F O/O/S YK	O/O/S YK
O/O/S YK 1A31 1S77		O/O/S HA 1E29 1A45	A/V HA 1E35	1S12 TO ED 0G00 TO CARS 1A55 TO ED 'EO'		1C86 0G00 TO HA A/V HA	O/O/S YK 0L01 TO THIRSK 0L01 TO YK (TRIAL RUN) A/V YK 'OE'	1A08 1L44 1A34
A/V HA 1E35		A/V FP 1S60 TO ED	A/V FP 1L44 1A34	1E48 1L43 1A31 'EO'		1C91 1G44 1A38 1G20 1E39 TO NCL	A/V YK 'OE'	1L41 1A22 1D08 5L04
A/V FP 1N14		1S70 TO LEUCHARS E/F (FIRE) 0G00 TO HA O/O/S HA	A/V FP 1L44 1A34	O/O/S FP 'EO'		E/F AT SCREM-ERSTON 37 149 ASSIST TO NCL O/O/S GD 1A40	A/V YK 'OE'	O/O/S YK
1E40 A/V FP		O/O/S HA	1L43 1A31	1S12 TO ED 1A38 1G20 'EO'		O/O/S FP 1S60 TO PE E/F O/O/S PE	A/V YK 'OE'	O/O/S YK
1L41 1A10 1S77		O/O/S HA	1L42 1A19	A/V HA 'EO'		O/O/S PE 'OE'	O/O/S YK 'OE'	O/O/S YK
A/V HA 1E35		O/O/S HA	1S12 TO ED O/O/S HA A/V HA 'EO'	1E48 O/O/S FP 1S70 TO ED 'EO'		O/O/S PE 'OE'	O/O/S YK A/V YK 'OE'	O/O/S YK
1L41 1A22 O/O/S FP 'OE'		O/O/S HA TOWED TO YK BY 47522 O/O/S YK	1E48 TO YK E/F O/O/S YK 'EO'	5Z20 TO ABDN 0Z20 TO HA O/O/S HA 1C95 0G00 TO HA 'EO'		1B26 A/V FP 'OE'	A/V YK 0B06 TO PE 0L22 TO KX 1L22 'OE'	O/O/S YK
5B26 1B26 (E/F AT WOOD GREEN 31 292 ASSIST TO KX) O/O/S FP'OE'		O/O/S YK	O/O/S YK 'EO'	1E48 A/V FP 1S70 TO ED 'EO'		1N12* O/O/S GD 1A40 TO DR E/F 'OE'	0L01 TO HO 0B02 TO FP A/V FP 1L22 'OE'	O/O/S YK
O/O/S FP 'OE'		O/O/S YK	1E43 TO DR (E/FatDAW LANE 08115 ASSIST TO DR) O/O/S DR 1A34 'EO'	O/O/S HA 1C86 1G44 1E26 'EO'		O/O/S DR 0B01 TO KX O/O/S KX 'OE'	0L01 TO HO O/O/S HO 1A41 TO DR (E/FatWKW 25083 ASSTTODR) 'OE'	1M62 1E99 O/O/S YK
O/O/S FP 'OE'		O/O/S YK	1S12 TO ED 1E26 'EO'	1A08 1S70 'EO'		O/O/S KX 'OE'	O/O/S DR 1E35 A/V FP 'OE'	O/O/S YK
O/O/S FP 'OE'		O/O/S YK	1A08 1L44 'EO'	A/V HA 1E61 12.25 ED-KX (ADDITIONAL) 'EO'		O/O/S KX 'OE'	O/O/S FP 'OE'	O/O/S YK

	55.002	55.004	55.007	55.008	55.009	55.010	55.011
SUNDAY 20 DECEMBER	A/V YK 1M70 1E50	YK W	O/O/S YK A/V YK 'OE'	1Z98 ED-CARS 0G00 TO HA 'EO'	A/V SF	A/V YK 'OE'	
MONDAY 21 DECEMBER	O/O/S YK	YK W	O/O/S YK A/V YK 1A22 1S77 TO YK	1E48 O/O/S FP 1S70 TO ED 'EO'	0B02 TO FP 1L43 O/O/S YK	0B06 TO PE O/O/S PE 'OE'	
TUESDAY 22 DECEMBER	O/O/S YK	YK W	E/F O/O/S YK 1A08 1L44 1A34	A/V HA 'EO'	O/O/S YK	O/O/S PE TOWED TO DR BY 55016 'OE'	
WEDNESDAY 23 DECEMBER	O/O/S YK	YK W	1S12 TO ED O/O/S HA 1E40	5F52CY-DUNDEE 1E52 1S70 TO ED 'EO'	O/O/S YK	O/O/S DR 0B02 TO FP (WITH 55016) 1L22 TO DR 'OE'	

Below:
On 29 December 55.009 *Alycidon* arrives at Peterborough with the 'Deltic Executive' railtour, the final private charter train using a Class 55. *C. J. Tuffs*

55.013	55.014	55.015	55.016	55.017	55.018	55.019	55.021	55.022
O/O/S FP 'OE'		O/O/S YK	A/V YK 'EO'	1L42 A/V YK 'EO'		O/O/S FP 'OE'	O/O/S FP 'OE'	1M69 1E22
FP W		O/O/S YK	1A08 TO PE E/F O/O/S PE 'EO'	5B26 YK TO PE 1B26 1L44 1A34 'EO'		O/O/S FP 'OE'	O/O/S FP 'OE'	O/O/S YK
FP W		O/O/S YK	O/O/S PE 0D00 TO DR TOWING 55010 O/O/S DR 'EO'	1S12 1E26 'EO'		O/O/S FP 1L22 TO LS 'EO'	O/O/S FP 'OE'	O/O/S YK
		1M62 1E99 O/O/S YK	O/O/S DR 0B02 TO FP (WITH 55010) 1D08 5L04 'EO'	1A08 1L44 1A34 'EO'		O/O/S HO 0D00 TO DR O/O/S DR 'OE'	O/O/S FP 'OE'	O/O/S YK

Below:
55.015 with the 'Hadrian Flyer' railtour at Bell Busk on Saturday 5 December.   *J. Fozard*

	55.002	55.004	55.007	55.008	55.009	55.010	55.011
THURSDAY 24 DECEMBER	O/O/S YK	YK W	A/V FP	A/V HA 1054 1O61 A/V HA 'EO'	1M62 1E99	E/FatCORBY GLEN 1S77 Pushed train TO GM 37 137 ASSISTED TO DR *	
FRIDAY 25 DECEMBER	O/O/S YK	YK W	A/V FP	A/V HA 'EO'	A/V YK	DR WKS W	
SATURDAY 26 DECEMBER	O/O/S YK	YK W	A/V FP	A/V HA 'EO'	A/V YK	DR WKS W	
SUNDAY 27 DECEMBER	O/O/S YK	YK W	1L42 O/O/S YK 1A19	5E27 'EO'	1M69 1E22		
MONDAY 28 DECEMBER	O/O/S YK	YK W	1L41 O/O/S YK	A/V FP 1S70 TO ED 'EO'	1E43 1L44 1A34		
TUESDAY 29 DECEMBER	O/O/S YK	YK W	O/O/S YK	1C86 1G44 1A38 1G20 'EO'	1G06 TO YK 1G06 TO KX 1S79 TO ED 'EO'		
WEDNESDAY 30 DECEMBER	1M53 1E98 O/O/S NRM 'OE'	YK W	1A08 (E/F AT DR, 47146 ASSISTED TO KX) O/O/S FP	1E48 O/O/S FP 'EO'	1M04 TO NCL E/F O/O/S GD 1A40		
THURSDAY 31 DECEMBER	O/O/S NRM 'OE'	YK W	O/O/S FP TOWED TO YK BY 31.121 O/O/S YK	O/O/S FP 'EO'	O/O/S FP		
FRIDAY 1 JANUARY	O/O/S NRM 'OE'	YK W	YK W	FP W	0B00 TO PE A/V PE		
SATURDAY 2 JANUARY	O/O/S NRM 'OE'	YK W	YK W	FP W	0G50 TO NCL 0G50 TO PE 0G50 TO YK		
SUNDAY 3 JANUARY	NRM W	YK W	YK W	FP W	YK W		
MONDAY 4 JANUARY	NRM W	YK W	Towed to Dr Wks with 55019/21 by 46009 W	FP W	YK W		
TUESDAY 5 JANUARY	NRM W	Towed to Dr Wks BY 47186 W	DR WKS W	FP W	Towed to Dr Wks with 55015/16/22 by 47552 W		

* TOWED TO DR WKS BY 55.019

55.013	55.014	55.015	55.016	55.017	55.018	55.019	55.021	55.022
FP W		O/O/S YK	O/O/S YK 'EO'	1S12 1E26 'EO'		O/O/S DR 0L01 TO YK 1A31 TO DR E/F O/O/S DR 'OE'	1N12 A/V GD 'OE'	O/O/S YK
FP W		O/O/S YK	O/O/S YK 'EO'	A/V YK 'EO'		A/V DR 'OE'	A/V GD 'OE'	O/O/S YK
FP W		O/O/S YK	O/O/S YK 'EO'	A/V YK 'EO'		A/V DR 'OE'	A/V GD 'OE'	O/O/S YK
FP W		1M70 1E50	O/O/S YK 'EO'	O/O/S YK 'EO'		O/O/S DR 'OE'	A/V GD 'OE'	O/O/S YK
FP V		O/O/S YK	O/O/S YK 'EO'	O/O/S YK 'EO'		O/O/S DR 'OE'	1F50 0050NCL-YK 0F50 TO NCL 1S60 TO ED 1E52 'OE'	O/O/S YK
P V		O/O/S YK	O/O/S YK 'EO'	1A08 1L44 1A34 'EO'		O/O/S DR 'OE'	1N00 1S08 1E52 'OE'	O/O/S YK
P V		O/O/S YK	O/O/S YK 'EO'	1S12 TO ED A/V HA 'EO'		0B00 TO GM (WITH 46009) 0B02 TO FP 1L43 0B00 TO FP 'OE'	1N12 1S14 1E35 'OE'	O/O/S YK 1A26 O/O/S FP
P		O/O/S YK 1A26 A/V FP	YK W	1E48/1L44 TO GM 1G26 to Knebworth E/F 5G26 TO KX TOWED BY 47426 'EO'		1N12 1S14 1E26 'OE'	1L41 O/O/S YK 'OE'	1S12 TO ED A/V HA
P		A/V FP	YK W	FP W		YK W	YK W	A/V HA
		1F50 TO ED 0F50 TO YK	YK W	FP W		YK W	YK W	1F50 TO KX 0F50 TO YK
		YK W	YK W	FP W		YK W	YK W	YK W
		YK W	YK W	FP W		Towed to Dr Wks with 55007/21 by 46009 W	Towed to Dr Wks WITH 55007/19 BY 46009 W	YK W
		Towed to Dr Wks with 55009/16/22 by 47552 W	Towed to Dr Wks with 55009/15/22 by 47552 W	FP W		DR WKS W	DR WKS W	Towed to Dr Wks with 55009/15/16 by 47 552 W

4 'Deltic' Railtours

Date	Locomotive	Headcode	Title and route
10/10/81	55.002	1Z73	*'Two Firths Express'* York-Edinburgh-York
17/10/81	55.009	1F52	Newcastle-Perth (light engine to Aberdeen)-Aberdeen-Newcastle
17/10/81	55.015	1Z47	*'Wessex Deltic'* Finsbury Park-Bournemouth-Eastleigh-Portsmouth-Finsbury Park
17/10/81	55.021	1Z42	*'Minsterman'* York-Scarborough-York
24/10/81	55.015	1F50	*'Deltic Salute'* York-Aberdeen-York
31/10/81	55.002	1F52	*'Celtic Deltic'* Kings Cross-Edinburgh-Peterborough
07/11/81	55.015	1F51	*'Deltic Queen of Scots'* Kings Cross-Edinburgh
07/11/81	55.002	1F51	*'Deltic Queen of Scots'* Edinburgh-Kings Cross
14/11/81	55.009	1Z37	*'Deltic Cumbrian'* Kings Cross-Leeds-Carlisle-Newcastle-Kings Cross
21/11/81	55.002	1Z10	*'Deltic Scotsman'* York-Carlisle-Newcastle-Inverkeithing-Edinburgh
21/11/81	55.013	1Z10	*'Deltic Scotsman'* Edinburgh-Bradford Exchange-York
28/11/81	55.009	1Z11	Newcastle-Carlisle-Edinburgh-Newcastle
28/11/81	55.016	1Z40	*'Deltic Devonian'* Finsbury Park-Exeter-Salisbury-Clapham-Liverpool Street
28/11/81	55.022	1Z38	*'Deltic Venturer'* York-Gloucester-Paddington-Worcester-York
05/12/81	55.015	1Z35	*'The Hadrian Flyer'* Peterborough-Carlisle-Newcastle-Peterborough
12/12/81	55.002	1G06	Norwich-York-Norwich
12/12/81	55.009	1Z55	*'Grampian Deltic'* Edinburgh-Aberdeen-Edinburgh
19/12/81	55.009	1G10	*'Deltic Broadsman'* Kings Cross-Grantham-Sleaford-Norwich-Ipswich-Liverpool Street
19/12/81	55.002	1Z25	*'Napier North-Eastern'* York-Scarborough-Bridlington-Doncaster
29/12/81	55.009	1G06	*'Deltic Executive'* Kings Cross-Harrogate-York-Hull-Doncaster-Kings Cross
02/01/82	55.015	1F50	*'Deltic Scotsman Farewell'* Kings Cross-Edinburgh
02/01/82	55.022	1F50	*'Deltic Scotsman Farewell'* Edinburgh-Kings Cross

Below:
No 55.009 *Alycidon* at Carlisle after arrival with the 'Deltic Cumbrian' railtour on 14 November 1981.
J. Sparks

5 Details and Dimensions of the 'Deltic'

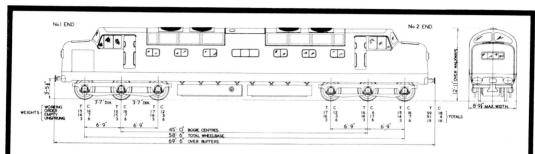

Built: English Electric Co Ltd; Vulcan Foundry, Newton-Le-Willows
Engine: Two D18/25s
Axle layout: Co-Co
Maximum permitted speed: 100mph
Brakes, locomotive: Straight air/automatic air
Brakes, train: Automatic air/air continuous vacuum
Train heating: Spanner Mk II boiler and electric from main generator
Wheelbase of bogie: 13ft 6in
Wheelbase of locomotive: 58ft 0in
Distance between bogie centres: 45ft 0in
Driving wheel diameter: New 43in, minimum permissible 40.5in
Length over buffers: 69ft 6in
Maximum width: 8ft 9½in
Maximum height: 12ft 10in
Minimum curve negotiable: 4 chains
Weight in working order as built: 99tons
Weight empty as built: 94tons 8cwt
Engine cylinder bore: 130mm
Engine cylinder stroke: 184mm
Compression ratio: 14:1
Fuel tank capacity: 900gal
Water tank capacity: 640gal
Maximum tractive effort: 57,500lb
Continuous tractive effort: 30,000lb
Continuous rail hp: 2,640
Boiler: Spanner Mk II
Pressure: 80lb/sq in
Steaming capacity: 2,450lb/hr

Power Unit
Engines (two): Napier Deltic D18/25
Cylinders: 18
Bore: 5.125in
Stroke: 7.25 x 2ins
Full load rating: 1,650hp at 1.500 rpm
Fuel capacity: 900gal
Fuel injection pump: CAV.F.M. 110 AYS
Fuel injector: CAV.BKB. 355 5074M
Transmission: Electric
Gear ratios: 53/18
Generator: EE 829A
Auxiliary generator: EE 913A
Traction motors: EE 538A (6)
Compressors: Worth-Simp MSV 38
Exhausters: Reaneu FRU
Batteries: DP Battery 48 RK – 192M/4
Battery capacity: 123 amp/hr
Battery nominal voltage: 110

Below :
55.022 *Royal Scots Grey* at York depot on 3 November 1981. *P. Gash*

6 Individual Deltic Information

55.001
Original BR number: D9001
EE works number: 2906
Vulcan Foundry Number; D558
Date to traffic: 23/02/61
Name: *St Paddy*
Origin of name: Racehorse, won Derby and St Leger 1960
Date and place of naming: 07/61, Doncaster
Allocations: FP, HA 03/12/67, FP 16/06/68
Air brakes fitted: 29/03/68
ETH fitted: 26/03/71
Re-painted from green to blue livery: mid-1969
Renumbered: W/E 23/02/74
Last train: 1S16 08.00 Kings Cross-Edinburgh (to Doncaster) 24/03/78
Reason for withdrawal: Two power-units required, surplus to requirements
Withdrawal date: 05/01/80
Where withdrawn: Doncaster Works
Disposal: Cut up at Doncaster Works 02/80

Below :
As 9001, *Saint Paddy* works wrong line at Morpeth during Sunday engineering work in 1969. *K. Morton*

Bottom:
55.001 near York on 29 August 1977 at the head of the 11.00 Kings Cross-Edinburgh. *C. J. Tuffs*

55.002
Original BR number: D9002
EE works numbers: 2907
Vulcan Foundry number: D559
Date to Traffic: 09/03/61
Name: *The Kings Own Yorkshire Light Infantry*
Origin of name: LNER 'V2' No 60872
Date and place of naming: 04/04/63, York
Allocations: GD, YK 13/05/79
Air brakes fitted: 24/11/67
ETH fitted: 04/05/71
Re-painted: 10/66
Renumbered: W/E 08/12/73 at Doncaster Works
Last train: 1E98 12.05 Liverpool-York 30/12/81
Reason for withdrawal: Life expired
Withdrawal date: 02/01/82
Where withdrawn: NRM annexe
Disposal: Preserved at the NRM in York

Below:
No 9002 leaving Kings Cross on 10 August 1971 with the 16.00 train to Edinburgh. The locomotive was dedicated to the National Railway Museum in a ceremony there on 12 December 1980, the green livery being paid for by the 'Friends of the NRM'. *J. H. Cooper-Smith*

Above:
In August 1981 British Rail ran two 'Merrymaker' trains from Newcastle to Whitby, both hauled by 55.002. This picture shows *The King's Own Yorkshire Light Infantry* about to run round its train at Battersby on the second charter on the 30th. *I. M. Flynn*

55.003
Original BR Number: D9003
EE works number: 2908
Vulcan Foundry number: D560
Date to traffic: 27/03/61
Name: *Meld*
Origin of name: Racehorse, won St Leger and 1,000 Guineas 1955
Date and place of naming: 07/61, Doncaster
Allocations: FP, HA 03/12/67, FP 16/06/68
Air brakes fitted: 14/02/68
ETH fitted: 05/12/70
Re-painted: 12/67
Renumbered: W/E 23/02/74
Last train: 1S27 07.22 Plymouth-Edinburgh (from York-Newcastle) 29/12/80
Reason for withdrawal: Overdue intermediate overhaul, surplus to requirements
Withdrawal date: 31/12/80
Where withdrawn: York depot
Disposal: Cut up at Doncaster Works 03/81

Above:
55.003 at Cleethorpes on 16 August 1980 with the 17.43 to Kings Cross. *Meld* was taken out of traffic at York at 23.00 on 29 December 1980 for attention to number two engine. Following inspection the next day it was found that the primary fan shaft was seriously damaged. As the locomotive was booked for withdrawal on 4 January 1981 because it was overdue for an overhaul at Doncaster Works, it was condemned in order to provide parts for 55.014 undergoing a 'D' exam, and so *Meld* was denied its planned finale of working the final down 'Hull Executive' on Friday 2 January.   *K. Alison*

Below:
55.003 departs Kings Cross in style on 14 May 1979, with the inaugural 17.05 'Hull Executive' train, at the time the fastest locomotive-hauled train in Britain. *Meld* was the first 'Deltic' to receive white cab surrounds, in early April 1979, prior to working the 'Northumbrian Ltd' railtour.
R. Newling-Goode

55.004
Original BR number: D9004
EE works number: 2909
Vulcan foundry number: D561
Date to traffic: 18/05/61
Name: *Queen's Own Highlander*
Origin of name: Regimental name, not previously carried by a locomotive
Date and place of naming: 23/05/64, Inverness
Allocations: HA, YK 13/05/79
Air brakes fitted: 12/01/68
ETH fitted: 27/08/71
Re-painted: 01/68
Renumbered: W/E 01/05/74
Last train: 1M76 15.50 York-Liverpool 28/10/81
Reason for withdrawal: To provide a power unit for 55.008
Withdrawal date: 01/11/81
Where withdrawn: Stratford TRS
Disposal: Cut up at Doncaster Works 07/83

Right:
55.004 heads north from Newcastle on 18 July 1981. The locomotive almost succumbed to the fate of 55.001 and 55.020 at Doncaster Works following a lengthy stay from 14 June 1978 to 2 December 1979, and even after all this time was not given a classified repair. *T. J. Ermel*

Below:
The 04.05 Kings Cross-Leeds train was supposed to be diagrammed for 'Deltic' haulage, one of the rare days on which a 'Deltic' was in fact used was 2 August 1980. 55.004 is seen here departing platform eight at Doncaster with the featherweight three-coach load. *P. M. Marsh*

55.005
Original BR number: D9005
EE works number: 2910
Vulcan Foundry number: D562
Date to traffic: 25/05/61
Name: *The Prince of Wales's Own Regiment of Yorkshire*
Origin of name: Regimental name, not previously carried by a locomotive
Date and place of naming: 08/10/63 York
Allocations: GD, YK 13/05/79
Air brakes fitted: 25/04/68
ETH fitted: 17/04/71
Re-painted: 09/69
Renumbered: Gateshead 25/01/74
Last train: 1E24 22.50 (29/01/81) Shrewsbury-York (from Leeds), 30/01/81
Reason for withdrawal: Due intermediate overhaul, surplus to requirements
Withdrawal date: 08/02/81
Where withdrawn: York depot
Disposal: Cut up at Doncaster Works, 02/83

Below:
55.005 poses outside York depot on 11 November 1980 prior to working the '150th Anniversary of Mail by Rail' commemorative train. *L. P. Gater*

Bottom:
55.005 at Edinburgh Waverley on 18 October 1980 with the 22.30 to Kings Cross. The locomotive was taken out of traffic at 05.00 on 30 January 1981 at York depot to undergo a 'B' exam, and withdrawn from service at 10.40 on 3 February 1981. Number one engine needed another secondary fan shaft fitted, and as the locomotive was booked for withdrawal on 8 February 1981, it was not practical to wait for the part to arrive. *I. M. Flynn*

55.006
Original BR number: D9006
EE works number: 2911
Vulcan Foundry number: D563
Date to traffic: 29/06/61
Name: *The Fife and Forfar Yeomanry*
Origin of name: Regimental name, not previously carried by a locomotive
Date and place of naming: 05/12/64 Leuchars
Allocations: GD, YK 13/05/79
Air brakes fitted: 25/04/68
ETH fitted: 05/03/71
Re-painted: 08/69
Renumbered: Gateshead 06/03/74
Last train: 5E74 19.00 Newcastle-York 06/02/81
Reason for withdrawal: Due intermediate overhaul, surplus to requirements
Withdrawal date: 08/02/81
Where withdrawn: York depot
Disposal: Cut up at Doncaster Works 07/81

Below:
55.006 enters Goole in the late evening of 27 May 1979 with the 17.05 Kings Cross-Hull train, the 'Hull Executive'. *P. M. Marsh*

Bottom:
55.006 arriving at Doncaster on 19 August 1979 with the 14.50 Newcastle-Doncaster train. The locomotive was stopped for repairs at York at 20.30 on 6 February 1981, and a decision taken for withdrawal just half an hour later because it was booked for condemnation on 8 February 1981, being due an intermediate repair. *B. Morrison*

55.007
Original BR number: D9007
EE works number: 2912
Vulcan Foundry number: D564
Date to traffic: 22/06/61
Name: *Pinza*
Origin of name: Racehorse, won Derby and King George VI and
Queen Elizabeth Stakes 1953
Date and place of naming: 22/06/61 Doncaster
Allocations: FP, YK 31/05/80
Air brakes fitted: 11/04/68
ETH fitted: 08/12/71
Re-painted: 11/67
Renumbered: W/E 16/02/74
Last train: 1A08 08.07 York-Kings Cross (failed at Doncaster)
30/12/81
Reason for withdrawal: Both power-units inoperative
Withdrawal date: 31/12/81
Where withdrawn: York depot
Disposal: Cut up at Doncaster Works 08/82

Above:
55.007 leaving Hull Paragon on 9 May 1981 with the
09.33 service to Kings Cross. This locomotive, along
with 55.001, was used for dynamic tests on dipped rail
joints between Cholsey and Didcot in January 1975.
C. R. Anthony

Below:
55.007 leaving Newcastle on 1 September 1977 with the
15.00 Edinburgh-Kings Cross train – the 'Silver
Jubilee'. *D. B. Stacey*

55.008
Original BR number: D9008
EE works number: 2913
Vulcan Foundry number: D565
Date to traffic: 07/07/61
Name: *The Green Howards*
Origin of name: LMS 'Royal Scot' No 6133 (different version from *The Green Howard*)
Date and place of naming: 30/09/63 Darlington
Allocations: GD, YK 13/05/79
Air brakes fitted: 17/05/68
ETH fitted: 02/10/71
Re-painted: 07/67
Renumbered: GD 31/01/74
Last train: 1E48 21.20 Aberdeen-Kings Cross (from Edinburgh) 29/12/81
Reason for withdrawal: Life expired
Withdrawal date: 31/12/81
Where withdrawn: Finsbury Park
Disposal: Cut up at Doncaster Works 08/82

Right:
A powerful photograph of 55.008, seen here passing Gateshead on 27 July 1974.   *T. J. Ermel*

Below:
The Green Howards, the only 'Deltic' to carry its crests until the end of service, waits for the right away at Darlington on 27 May 1981.   *T. J. Ermel*

55.009
Original BR number: D9009
EE works number: 2914
Vulcan Foundry number: D566
Date to traffic: 21/07/61
Name: *Alycidon*
Origin of name: Racehorse, second in St Leger 1948, won Ascot Gold
Cup and Goodwood Cup 1949
Date and place of naming: 21/07/61 Doncaster
Allocations: FP, HA 03/12/67, FP 16/06/68, YK 31/05/80
Air brakes fitted: 14/06/68
ETH fitted: 17/10/70
Re-painted: 05/68
Renumbered: W/E 26/01/74
Last train: 1A40 21.00 Newcastle-King Cross 30/12/81
Reason for withdrawal: Life expired
Withdrawal date: 02/01/82
Where withdrawn: York depot
Disposal: Preserved by the 'Deltic' Preservation Society on the North
Yorkshire Moors Railway

Below:
Three weeks after 55.002's visit to the Nene Valley
Railway, 55.009 became the second 'Deltic' to visit the
line with the 'Deltic Fenman II' railtour on 25 May 1981.
Here we see the locomotive passing a gantry of signals
(used by BR for sighting tests) on the Fletton loop.
R. Harrison

55.010
Original BR number: D9010
EE works number: 2915
Vulcan Foundry number: D567
Date to traffic: 24/07/61
Name: *The King's Own Scottish Borderer*
Origin of name: LMS 'Royal Scot' No 6104 (different version from *Scottish Borderer*)
Date and place of naming: 08/05/65 Dumfries
Allocations: HA, YK 13/05/79
Air brakes fitted: 01/02/68
ETH fitted: 07/11/70
Re-painted: 02/68
Renumbered: W/E 16/06/74
Last train: 1L22 23.00 Kings Cross-Bradford (failed at Grantham) 23/12/81
Reason for withdrawal: Both power-units inoperative
Withdrawal date: 24/12/81
Where withdrawn: Doncaster Works
Disposal: Cut up at Doncaster Works 05/82

Below:
55.010 makes an energetic start from Grantham on 25 July 1980 with the 09.35 Hull-Kings Cross train. One nameplate had to be taken off the locomotive because of attempted removal by vandals. *R. Newling-Goode*

Above:
55.010 arriving at Doncaster on 2 May 1978 with the 11.00 Kings Cross-Edinburgh train. This locomotive worked the last booked 'Deltic'-hauled down 'Flying Scotsman' on 6 May 1978. *A. O. Wynn*

55.011
Original BR number: D9011
EE works number: 2916
Vulcan Foundry number: D568
Date to traffic: 24/08/61
Name: *The Royal Northumberland Fusiliers*
Origin of name: Regimental name, not previously carried by a locomotive
Date and place of naming: 28/05/63 Newcastle
Allocations: GD, YK 13/05/79
Air brakes fitted: 08/07/68
ETH fitted: 06/08/71
Re-painted: 07/68
Renumbered: W/E 16/02/74
Last train: 1A45 22.55 Newcastle-Kings Cross 5/11/81
Reason for withdrawal: To provide a power-unit for 55.022
Withdrawal date: 08/11/81
Where withdrawn: Stratford TRS
Disposal: Cut up at Doncaster Works 12/82

Below:
'Deltics' at Scarborough on summer Saturdays brought a welcome change of scenery in the final years. 55.011 *The Royal Northumberland Fusiliers* eases away with a 12.00 additional service to Glasgow Queen Street on 2 August 1980. This locomotive was the only 'Deltic' involved in a major accident, at Morpeth in 1969 when the train took the curve at too high a speed. The engine was the only vehicle to remain on the track, and six people were killed. *J. Fielding*

55.012
Original BR number: D9012
EE works number: 2917
Vulcan Foundry number: D569
Date to traffic: 04/09/61
Name: *Crepello*
Origin of name: Racehorse, won Derby and 2,000 Guineas 1957
Date and place of naming: 04/09/61 Doncaster
Allocations: FP, HA 03/12/67, FP 16/06/68
Air brakes fitted: 20/03/68
ETH fitted: 12/01/71
Re-painted: 03/68
Renumbered: W/E 02/02/74
Last train: 1E39 22.25 Edinburgh-Kings Cross 13/5/81
Reason for withdrawal: Overdue intermediate overhaul, surplus to requirements
Withdrawal date: 31/05/81
Where withdrawn: Finsbury Park
Disposal: Cut up at Doncaster Works 09/81

Below:
Twelve days after withdrawal a forlorn looking *Crepello* stands inside York shed waiting for its last journey to Doncaster Works. 55.012 was taken out of traffic at Finsbury Park at 07.30 on 14 May 1981 to undergo a 'C' exam, and a decision to withdraw it was taken on 18 May as it was due to be condemned, being well overdue an intermediate overhaul at Doncaster. The locomotive was towed to York on 20 May by 31.262 to be cannibalised. *P. E. Gash*

Bottom:
55.012 accelerates through Selby and heads south with an Edinburgh-Kings Cross relief in the summer of 1980. This locomotive worked the 'East Coast Pullman Salute' on 20 May 1978, the official farewell Pullman service on the Eastern Region. *P. M. Marsh*

55.013
Original BR number: D9013
EE works number: 2918
Vulcan Foundry number: D570
Date to traffic: 14/09/61
Name: *The Black Watch*
Origin of name: LMS 'Royal Scot' No 6102 (different version from *Black Watch*)
Date and place of naming: 16/01/63 Dundee
Allocation: HA, FP 25/02/68, HA 16/06/68, YK 13/05/79
Air brakes fitted: 18/12/68
ETH fitted: 15/05/71
Re-painted: 02/68
Renumbered: W/E 28/02/74
Last train: 1B26 07.23 Peterborough-Kings Cross (failed at Wood Green) 16/12/81
Reason for withdrawal: Both power-units inoperative
Withdrawal date: 20/12/81
Where withdrawn: Finsbury Park
Disposal: Cut up at Doncaster Works December 1982

Right:
55.013 *The Black Watch* arrives at Inverkeithing on a Dundee-Kings Cross working on 8 August 1980.
I. M. Flynn

Below:
55.013 slows for the Dunbar stop on the 05.50 Kings Cross-Aberdeen train on 12 September 1981. York depot staff specially prepared *The Black Watch* to take part in the 'Rocket 150' celebration at Rainhill, but *Tulyar* was chosen much to their disappointment.
D. M. MacCorquodale

55.014
Original BR number: D9014
EE works number: 2919
Vulcan Foundry number: D571
Date to traffic: 29/09/61
Name: *The Duke of Wellington's Regiment*
Origin of name: LMS 'Royal Scot' No 6145 (different version from
Wellington's Regiment [West Riding])
Date and place of naming: 20/10/63 Doncaster
Allocations: GD YK 13/05/79
Air brakes fitted: 06/06/68
ETH fitted: 23/07/71
Re-painted: 11/69
Renumbered: Gateshead 29/01/74
Last train: 1S14 08.10 Newcastle-Edinburgh (failed at Cramlington)
10/11/81
Reason for withdrawal: To provide spares
Withdrawal date: 22/11/81
Where withdrawn: York depot
Disposal: Cut up at Doncaster Works 02/82

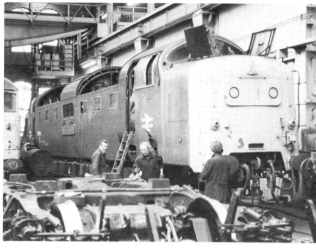

Above:
55.014 undergoing its final 'light' repair at Doncaster
Works on 25 November 1979. In January 1980 'The
Duke' made two unusual outings: on the 18th it towed
47.305 and 40.147 to Crewe Works, and on the 22nd it
towed 46.035 to Derby Works. The locomotive was
restricted to one engine at the time, waiting acceptance
by Doncaster Works. *R. Athey*

Below:
55.014 makes its way on to the main line after calling at
Doncaster with the 09.36 Hull-Kings Cross train on 30
April 1981. 'The Duke's' last appearance of note was at
Old Oak Common open day on 20 September 1981.
C. R. Davis

55.015
Original BR number: D9015
EE works number: 2920
Vulcan Foundry number: D572
Date to traffic: 13/10/61
Name: *Tulyar*
Origin of name: Racehorse, won Derby, St Leger and Eclipse Stakes 1952
Date and place of naming: 13/10/61 Doncaster
Allocations: FP, YK 31/05/80
Air brakes fitted: 22/02/68
ETH fitted: 13/02/71
Re-painted: 11/68
Renumbered: W/E 02/02/74
Last train: 1F50 08.30 Kings Cross-Edinburgh 'Deltic Scotsman Farewell' 02/01/82
Reason for withdrawal: Life expired
Withdrawal date: 02/01/82
Where withdrawn: York depot
Disposal: Privately preserved at the Midland Railway Trust, Butterley

Below:
A rare photograph of the first production 'Deltic' to visit Liverpool. 55.015 stands at Lime Street station after bringing in the 11.28 from Newcastle on 19 June 1979. *P. Calderly*

Bottom:
55.015 at Finsbury Park depot on 17 March 1981 after the 'Deltic' Preservation Society had presented the locomotive with a plaque commemorating its appearance in the Rainhill Calvacade of May 1980. It was this plaque which saved *Tulyar* from withdrawal in May 1981, despite being more overdue for overhaul than 55.012 *Crepello*. *R. Newling-Goode*

55.016
Original BR number: D9016
EE works number: 2921
Vulcan Foundry number: D573
Date to traffic: 27/10/61
Name: *Gordon Highlander*
Origin of name: LNER Class D40 and LMS 'Royal Scot' class
locomotive
Date and place of naming: 28/07/64 Aberdeen
Allocations: HA, FP 03/12/67, HA 16/06/68, YK 13/05/79
Air brakes fitted: 07/10/67
ETH fitted: 12/10/71
Re-painted: 10/67
Renumbered: W/E 16/03/74
Last train: 5L04 23.30 Hull-York 23/12/81
Reason for withdrawal: Defective power-unit and boiler
Withdrawal date: 30/12/81
Where withdrawn: York depot
Disposal: Preserved by Deltic 9000 Limited on the Nene Valley
Railway, Peterborough

Below:
55.016 at Leeds City station. This was the first 'Deltic' to
receive a 'general' repair at Doncaster Works. *British
Rail*

Bottom:
The LCGB North West Branch 'Deltic Discoverer' railtour
headed by 55.016 pauses at Hellifield on 27 October
1979. The 'Deltic' worked the tour from Leeds to
Glasgow and return – outward via Kilmarnock and back
via Beattock. *E. N. Bellass*

55.017
Original BR number: D9017
EE works number: 2922
Vulcan Foundry number: D574
Date to traffic: 05/11/61
Name: *The Durham Light Infantry*
Origin of name: LNER 'V2' No 60964
Date and place of naming: 20/11/61 Durham
Allocations: GD, YK 13/05/79
Air brakes fitted: 08/05/68
ETH fitted: 21/05/71
Repainted: 10/69
Renumbered: Gateshead 03/02/74
Last train: 1G26 18.58 Grantham-Kings Cross (failed at Knebworth) 31/12/81
Reason for withdrawal: Life expired
Withdrawal date: 31/12/81
Where withdrawn: Finsbury Park
Disposal: Cut up at Doncaster Works, 01/83

Above:
55.017 passing Huyton Quarry on 16 November 1979 in charge of the 14.05 Liverpool-Newcastle train.
J. S. Buckley

Below:
55.017 leaving York on 20 March 1981 with the 05.50 Kings Cross-Aberdeen train. *P. E. Gash*

55.018
Original BR number: D9018
EE works number: 2923
Vulcan Foundry number: D575
Date to traffic: 24/11/61
Name: *Ballymoss*
Origin of name: Racehorse, won St Leger, King George VI and Queen Elizabeth Stakes 1958
Date and place of naming: 24/11/61 Doncaster
Allocations: FP, YK 31/05/80
Air brakes fitted: 07/03/68
ETH fitted: 23/02/71
Re-painted: 05/69
Renumbered: W/E 09/02/74
Last train: 1D08 19.40 Kings Cross-Hull (failed at Doncaster) 12/10/81
Reason for withdrawal: To provide a power-unit for 55.008 (eventually given to 55.007)
Withdrawal date: 18/10/81
Where withdrawn: York depot
Disposal: Cut up at Doncaster Works 01/82

Below:
55.018 *Ballymoss*, one of the most popular members of the class, leaving York on 3 August 1981 with a Kings Cross working. The long lay-over time at York on these semi-fast services resulted in excessive exhaust fumes being emitted on departure, caused by lubricating oil building up in the collector drums of the power-units. Residents of the estates at Dringhouses complained, and this led to the instruction to drivers not to accelerate until they were past the houses. *T. J. Ermel*

55.019
Original BR number: D9019
EE works number: 2924
Vulcan Foundry number: D576
Date to traffic: 11/12/61
Name: *Royal Highland Fusilier*
Origin of name: Regimental name not previously carried by a locomotive
Date and place of naming: 11/09/65 Glasgow Central
Allocations: HA, FP 03/12/67. HA 16/06/68, YK 13/05/79
Air brakes fitted: 10/11/67
ETH fitted: 24/04/71
Re-painted: 04/68
Renumbered: W/E 22/11/73
Last train: 1E26 16.30 Aberdeen-York (from Edinburgh) 31/12/81
Reason for withdrawal: Life expired
Withdrawal date: 31/12/81
Where withdrawn: York depot
Disposal: Preserved by the Deltic Preservation Society on the North Yorkshire Moors Railway

Below:
55.019 passing Portobello on 4 June 1981 with the 17.18 Edinburgh-Newcastle stopping train. *Royal Highland Fusilier's* most unusual working in the final years was on 21 February 1979 when it worked the 13.57 Peterborough-Leicester train and 15.23 return because of a dmu failure. *I. M. Flynn*

55.020
Original BR number: D9020
EE works number: 2925
Vulcan Foundry number: D577
Date to traffic: 12/02/62
Name: *Nimbus*
Origin of name: Racehorse, won Derby and 2,000 Guineas 1949
Date and place of naming: 12/02/62 Doncaster
Allocations: FP
Air brakes fitted: 30/12/67
ETH fitted: 09/04/71
Re-painted: 03/68
Renumbered: W/E 10/11/73
Last train: 6E05 Oxford-Newcastle Parcels (from York) 29/03/78
Reason for withdrawal: Two power-units required, surplus to requirements
Withdrawal date: 05/01/80
Where withdrawn: Doncaster Works
Disposal: Cut up at Doncaster Works 01/80

Below:
55.020 in between duties at Edinburgh Waverley on 25 March 1978 – four days later its engines were silenced for ever. After being robbed of spares at Gateshead for 55.002, 55.020 was towed to Doncaster on 25 April, and was 'in works' from the 26th to await a power-unit. Like 55.001 *St Paddy, Nimbus* fell victim to a shortage of engines and was condemned on 18 December 1979; cutting up commenced on 8 January 1980. *K. Alison*

Bottom left:
55.020 *Nimbus* passing Low Fell on 11 August 1974 with a Kings Cross service. This locomotive was the only 'Deltic' to be allocated to one depot – Finsbury Park – for its entire life. *T. J. Ermel*

Bottom right:
Nimbus was the first 'Deltic' to be broken up. This is the locomotive in its heyday working the up 'Flying Scotsman' past Bensham on 2 March 1974. *T. J. Ermel*

55.021
Original BR number: D9021
EE works number: 2926
Vulcan Foundry number: D578
Date to traffic: 02/05/62
Name: *Argyll and Sutherland Highlander*
Origin of name: LMS 'Royal Scot' No 6107
Date and place of naming: 29/11/63 Stirling
Allocations: HA, FP 29/11/64, HA 26/06/65, YK 13/05/79
Air brakes fitted: 06/12/67
ETH fitted: 19/09/70
Re-painted: 12/67
Renumbered: W/E 02/01/74
Last train: 1L41 09.40 Kings Cross-York 31/12/81
Reason for withdrawal: Life expired
Withdrawal date: 31/12/81
Where withdrawn: York depot
Disposal: Cut up at Doncaster Works 09/82

Right:
In August 1981 British Rail ran two 'Merrymaker' excursions from Edinburgh to Oban using Mk 3 coaches. A 'Deltic' had to be used as Scottish Region Class 37s at that time were not fitted with ETH, and the heavy axles of Class 47s barred their use on the West Highland line. 55.021 was the locomotive used on both occasions, and it is seen here at Oban on the second 'West Highland Tour' on 23 August. *I. M. Flynn*

Below:
55.021 at Finsbury Park on 20 July 1975. *G. Scott-Lowe*

55.022

Original BR number: D9000
EE works number: 2905
Vulcan Foundry number: D557
Date to traffic: 28/02/61
Name: *Royal Scots Grey*
Origin of name: LMS 'Royal Scot' No 6101
Date and place of naming: 18/02/62 Edinburgh
Allocations: HA, FP 03/12/67, HA 16/06/68, YK 13/05/79
Air brakes fitted: 03/11/67
ETH fitted: 30/10/71
Re-painted: 11/67
Renumbered: W/E 10/04/74
Last train: 1F50 14.30 Edinburgh-Kings Cross 'Deltic Scotsman Farewell' 02/01/82
Reason for withdrawal: Life expired
Withdrawal date: 02/01/82
Where withdrawn: York depot
Disposal: Preserved by Deltic 9000 Limited on the Nene Valley Railway, Peterborough

Right:
The sun catches the exhaust fumes of 55.022 as it runs through Princes Street Gardens on 27 August 1981, on its way to Haymarket shed after working the 09.40 Kings Cross-Edinburgh train. *I. M. Flynn*

Below:
On a cold 28 February 1981, 55.022 enters Selby with the 12.20 Kings Cross-York service. The locomotive was adorned with a special headboard presented by the 'Deltic' Preservation Society to celebrate 20 years of service by 'Deltics' on the East Coast main line. High Speed Trains, which first ran on the Eastern Region on 20 March 1978, prevented the locomotive reaching its 21st anniversary. *P. M. Marsh*

7 Final 'Deltic' Light, Intermediate and General Repairs at Doncaster Works

Locomotive	Repair	Assignment date	In works	Ex works	To traffic
55.001	Intermediate	24/09/74 (ASAP)	25/09/74	05/11/74	05/11/74
	Light	14/10/75 (ASAP)	14/10/75	17/11/75	18/11/75
	Intermediate	18/11/76 (when 55.007 released)	26/11/76	27/02/77	28/02/77
55.002	Light	10/12/74	12/12/74	31/12/74	31/12/74
	General	16/03/76 (ASAP)	16/03/76	10/11/76	11/11/76
	Light	09/06/78 (when 55.013 released)	14/06/78	16/08/78	17/08/78
	Intermediate	10/10/80	14/10/80	28/11/80	11/12/80
55.003	Intermediate	30/04/74	01/05/74	02/08/74	03/08/74
	Light	31/07/75 (ASAP)	31/07/75	20/08/75	21/08/75
	Intermediate	14/10/76	18/10/76	31/12/76	—
	Rectification	—	01/01/77	14/01/77	14/01/77
	Light	15/01/79 (ASAP)	17/01/79	24/02/79	02/03/79
55.004	Intermediate	04/10/74	10/09/74	12/10/74	12/10/74
	Light	07/11/75 (ASAP)	08/11/75	28/11/75	28/11/75
	Intermediate	13/12/76	15/12/76	19/03/77	19/03/77
	Light	29/05/80	03/06/80	28/06/80	29/06/80
55.005	Intermediate	06/11/74 (ASAP)	07/11/74	09/12/74	09/12/74
	Light	28/01/76	29/01/76	12/02/76	12/02/76
	Intermediate	31/03/77 (ASAP)	31/03/77	21/10/77	—
	Rectification	—	24/10/77	26/10/77	26/10/77
	Light	28/06/79 (ASAP)	05/07/79	08/08/79	09/08/79
55.006	Intermediate	11/10/74	15/10/74	26/11/74	26/11/74
	Light	01/12/75 (ASAP)	03/12/75	18/12/75	18/12/75
	Intermediate	16/03/77	21/03/77	28/06/77	28/06/77
	Light	16/05/79 (ASAP)	18/05/79	21/06/79	21/06/79
55.007	Light	16/08/74	22/08/74	26/09/74	27/09/74
	Intermediate	18/08/75 (ASAP)	19/08/75	04/12/75	04/12/75
	Light	05/11/76 (when 55.002 released)	08/11/76	22/11/76	22/11/76
	Intermediate	14/07/78	17/07/78	25/11/78	26/11/78
	Light	27/08/80 (ASAP)	28/08/80	19/09/80	—
	Rectification	—	25/09/80	29/09/80	29/09/80
55.008	Light	07/02/74	11/02/74	20/02/74	—
	Intermediate	19/03/75 (ASAP)	20/03/75	07/09/75	07/09/75
	Light	22/09/76 (ASAP)	23/09/76	11/10/76	11/10/76
	Intermediate	09/03/78	15/03/78	03/08/78	03/08/78
	Light	31/07/80	06/08/80	26/08/80	27/08/80
55.009	Light	08/04/74	05/04/74	22/04/74	22/04/74
	Intermediate	07/03/75	11/03/75	05/02/76	05/02/76
	Light (in works already 31/01/77 No 2 P/U Deph)		31/01/77	20/02/77	20/02/77
	Intermediate	23/11/78 (ASAP)	01/12/78	24/03/79	25/03/79
	Light	19/11/80	24/11/80	19/12/80	19/12/80

Locomotive	Repair	Assignment date	In works	Ex works	To traffic
55.010	Light	25/07/75	29/07/75	08/08/75	08/08/75
	Intermediate	16/09/76	21/09/76	17/12/76	17/12/76
	Light	18/09/78 (ASAP)	23/09/78	24/10/78	24/10/78
	Intermediate	23/08/80 (ASAP)	28/08/80	17/10/80	17/10/80
55.011	Light	10/01/74	14/01/74	23/01/74	—
	Intermediate	29/01/75 (Already in works)	22/01/75	22/04/75	22/04/75
	Light	30/03/76 (Already in works)	25/03/76	24/06/76	24/06/76
	Intermediate	05/01/78	09/01/78	22/05/78	22/05/78
	Light	30/10/79	30/10/79	18/11/79	18/11/79
55.012	Light	24/08/73 (ASAP)	27/08/73	14/09/73	14/09/73
	Intermediate	17/09/74	18/09/74	30/10/74	30/10/74
	Light	17/11/75	18/11/75	01/12/76	01/12/76
	Intermediate	17/12/76	20/12/76	27/04/77	28/04/77
	Light	01/03/79 (Already in works)	01/03/79	31/03/79	01/04/79
55.013	Light	28/02/75 (Already in works)	20/01/75	09/05/75	09/05/75
	General	24/05/76	25/05/76	12/12/76	12/12/76
	Light	22/05/78 (Already in works)	13/05/78	14/06/78	15/06/78
	Intermediate	04/01/80	07/01/80	23/02/80	23/02/80
55.014	Intermediate	30/12/74 (Already in works)	30/12/74	19/03/75	19/03/75
	Light	15/04/76 (Already in works)	14/04/76	16/06/76	16/06/76
	Intermediate	08/12/77	12/12/77	28/04/78	28/04/78
	Light	19/11/79	23/11/79	10/12/79	11/12/79
55.015	Intermediate	12/07/74	13/07/74	10/09/74	11/09/74
	Light	02/10/75	06/10/75	21/10/75	21/10/75
	Intermediate	— (Already in works)	29/01/79	05/05/79	08/05/79
55.016	General	02/07/75	05/07/75	27/04/76	27/04/76
	Light	18/10/77 (ASAP)	19/10/77	10/11/77	10/11/77
55.017	Intermediate	22/11/74	26/11/74	11/03/75	11/03/75
	Light	03/03/76	12/03/76	26/03/76	26/03/76
	Intermediate	30/09/77	03/10/77	19/01/78	19/01/78
	Light	11/10/79 (ASAP)	16/10/79	02/11/79	—
	Rectification	—	03/11/79	10/11/79	10/11/79
55.018	Intermediate	— (Already in works)	11/11/74	21/03/75	21/03/75
	Light	24/02/76 (ASAP)	25/02/76	13/03/76	13/03/76
	Intermediate	30/06/77 (ASAP)	30/06/77	10/12/77	10/12/77
	Light	13/09/79 (ASAP)	14/09/79	10/10/79	11/10/79
55.019	Light	08/11/74	11/11/74	22/11/74	22/11/74
	General	22/01/76	27/01/76	22/09/76	22/09/76
	Light	27/04/78 (Already in works)	27/04/78	18/05/78	18/05/78
	Intermediate	09/04/80 (ASAP)	10/04/80	27/05/80	28/05/80
55.020	Light	29/10/74	30/10/74	08/11/74	08/11/74
	Intermediate	03/12/75	04/12/75	02/03/76	02/03/76
	Light	15/08/77	16/08/77	11/09/77	11/09/77
55.021	Light	18/12/74 (ASAP)	19/12/74	12/02/75	12/02/75
	General	— (Already in works)	22/04/76	31/12/76	—
	Rectification	—	01/01/77	19/01/77	19/01/77
	Light	26/03/79	28/03/79	26/04/79	27/04/79
55.022	Light	30/07/74 (ASAP)	30/07/74	28/08/74	28/08/74
	Intermediate	— (Already in works)	25/11/75	26/02/76	25/02/76
	Light	11/03/77	14/03/77	30/03/77	30/03/77
	Intermediate	12/07/79 (ASAP)	16/07/79	22/09/79	24/09/79

8
'Deltic' Demise
by C. S. Stubbs

It's a pleasing and romantic story
About the Deltics in their glory,
Their taking over ancient steam
Was just a part of all the dream.

It's sad to think the days will die
Of all the Deltics passing by,
No longer seen along our track
From Edinburgh, Kings Cross and back.

No longer will we hear the roar
Through tunnels, echoing their soar,
The bridges, cuttings, filing past
Absorbing all the engines' blast.

Their tasks performed with little strain
Those dual engines, power brain,
Exhaust prolific from their pores
Over hills and through the moors.

So proud they pass the signalbox
Or shunting yards and station clocks,
The smaller trains throughout the day
Conceded preference, right of way.

With destinations into sight
They stormed the day and lulled the night,
Triumphant in their willing chore
Like the 'iron horse' which went before.

That dull two-tone horn heard round the bend
Well-wishers with farewells to send,
Heads out of windows on the trip
The Deltic grinds its wheels to grip.

Withdrawal, it sadly draws so near
And silences enthusiasts' cheer,
Cassette tape sounds and camera shot
Will not be heard and soon forgot.

The strength and might of power on
Those halcyon days, alas are gone,
And heard above the dismantler's spree
The whisper of an HST.

'Tis now the death class fifty-five
The cutter's torch you won't survive,
Your reputation is unmarred,
Standing in the breaker's yard.